CHURCHILL'S ANGEL

CHURCHILL'S ANGEL

THE LIFE OF SIS AGENT HAZEL 'JICKY' SMITH

NICOLETTA MAGGI

Pen & Sword
MILITARY
AN IMPRINT OF PEN & SWORD BOOKS LTD.
YORKSHIRE – PHILADELPHIA

First published in Great Britain in 2025 by
Pen & Sword Military
An imprint of
Pen & Sword Books Ltd
Yorkshire - Philadelphia

Copyright © Nicoletta Maggi, 2025

ISBN 978 1 03612 970 5

The right of Nicoletta Maggi to be identified as the Author of this work has been asserted by her in accordance with the Copyright, Designs and Patents Act 1988.

A CIP catalogue record for this book is available from the British Library.

All rights reserved. No part of this book may be reproduced, transmitted, downloaded, decompiled or reverse engineered in any form or by any means, electronic or mechanical including photocopying, recording or by any information storage and retrieval system, without permission from the Publisher in writing. NO AI TRAINING: Without in any way limiting the Author's and Publisher's exclusive rights under copyright, any use of this publication to "train" generative artificial intelligence (AI) technologies to generate text is expressly prohibited. The Author and Publisher reserve all rights to license uses of this work for generative AI training and development of machine learning language models.

Typeset in INDIA by IMPEC eSolutions
Printed and bound in England by CPI Group (UK) Ltd, Croydon, CR0 4YY

The Publisher's authorised representative in the EU for product safety is Authorised Rep Compliance Ltd., Ground Floor, 71 Lower Baggot Street, Dublin D02 P593, Ireland.
www.arccompliance.com

For a complete list of Pen & Sword titles please contact:

PEN & SWORD BOOKS LIMITED
George House, Units 12 & 13, Beevor Street, Off Pontefract Road,
Barnsley, S71 1HN, UK
E-mail: enquiries@pen-and-sword.co.uk
Website: www.pen-and-sword.co.uk

or

PEN AND SWORD BOOKS
1950 Lawrence Rd, Havertown, PA 19083, USA
E-mail: Uspen-and-sword@casematepublishers.com
Website: www.penandswordbooks.com

'It is the memory, the soul of a people, that we want to pass on, and along with it, the interest in our very often forgotten traditions. We wanted to pass on to the young and the not-so-young documentary sources, which would otherwise have been lost, concerning our origins and the behaviour of so many people of the past, who, for various reasons, have left their distinguishing mark. With our writings, we also hope to leave, intra et extra moenia, a good memory of those of us who have dedicated part of our free time to the research of our cultural and historical heritage.'

Mario Maggi

Contents

Acknowledgements   ix
Preface   xi

Part One: Portrait of an Invisible Angel Against the Nazis

Chapter 1	Hazel or Jicky?	3
Chapter 2	To Paris with Love	6
Chapter 3	Write a Few Lines by Hand...	10
Chapter 4	Churchill and the Secret Service	17
Chapter 5	The Hermès Family	33
Chapter 6	Dear Paolo	41
Chapter 7	Codes, Acronyms and Numbers	51
Chapter 8	Jicky's Diaries and Personal Address Book	56
Chapter 9	Nicoletta, Nicole or Nico	73
Chapter 10	My Friend Dorothy	77
Chapter 11	Nazis	81
Chapter 12	Seize the Moment	84
Chapter 13	Confession	90
Chapter 14	The King's White Horse	94
Chapter 15	The Seven Lives	99

Part Two: The French Resistance: An In-Depth Investigation Using Jicky's Connections

Chapter 1	The Resistance: Imagine Spring!	109
Chapter 2	Bernard Buffet, the Expressionist Painter	116

Chapter 3	Jicky's Thoughts of Spring	122
Chapter 4	Desperately Seeking Gerard Vogel	129
Chapter 5	A French Identity Document with a London Stamp	132
Chapter 6	Resistance Fighters Lucien Durand and Gerard Vogel	136
Chapter 7	Lucienne Durand, Josephine Baker and the 18th Arrondissement	140
Chapter 8	Gerard Vogel in Prison	143
Chapter 9	The Mystery of Jicky's British Colleagues in the French Resistance	146
Chapter 10	The Disappearance and Discovery of Gerard Vogel	151

Part Three: Going Home: Jicky's Family, Town and Her Final Secrets

Chapter 1	Jicky's Hometown	158
Chapter 2	The Discovery of Jicky's Family	160
Chapter 3	Secret, Fairytale Harpenden	167
Chapter 4	No 95 Batford Prisoner of War Camp	172
Chapter 5	Another 'Enigma' Cracked by a British Engineer	174
Chapter 6	Anthony Piercey's Revelations	180
Chapter 7	A Plaque for Jicky	182

Bibliography 184
Endnotes 187
Index 191

Acknowledgements

I would like to thank Guy Dinmore, former correspondent of the *Financial Times* in Rome, for writing the original preface to *Churchill's Angel* and for coming to Italy from England especially for the first presentation of the book.

Crucial to my research in Harpenden was David Keen, curator of the Harpenden and District Local History Society, who I had contacted for information about Jicky, Hazel Smith, and her family. He immediately put me in touch with Diana Parrott, chair of the Harpenden and District Local History Society, who took steps to send me all the documentation on Jicky from their historical archives. When I visited Harpenden, Diana Parrott, together with the society's archivist, Rosemary Ross, showed me the essence of the town with a visit to the centre and especially to the house where Jicky was born. Rosemary also took me by car to see the historical realities around the town. Thanks to them, I was able to understand Jicky's birthplace and background first hand.

I would like to thank the former mayor of Harpenden, Nicola Linacre, for sending her greetings in a video to the participants who flocked to the square in Sirolo for the presentation of the Italian edition of *Churchill's Angel*.

For my research in France on Jicky's Resistance partner, I am grateful to Sylvain Cornil-Frerrot, Responsable des recherches historiques Fondation de la France Libre. He explained to me that their archives were not digitised and that I could contact them directly for my requests, whereupon they would give me the code for the files and I would have to contact the historical archive in Vincennes.

Essential for the French documentation in Vincennes was the contribution of David Sbrava, Attaché d'administration de l'Etat, Chef de la Division de l'accueil et de l'information du public (DAIP), Département des publics (DP), Centre historique des archives, who helped me find the files I was looking for.

For my research in France, I contacted the former Italian ambassador in Paris, Giandomenico Magliano, who very diligently put the cultural facilities and social affairs service of the embassy at my disposal.

Immediately after the publication of the Italian edition of *Churchill's Angel*, I contacted British intelligence historian Bernard O'Connor for further investigations for the new publication. He replied promptly, providing me with precise and fundamental information to help me understand the workings of the British intelligence services at that time. Afterwards, he proposed we write a book together and *Operation Etna: Britain's Infiltration of Soviet Agents into Italy* was published in 2023 in English and then in Italian.

I would like to thank Umberto Bossi, who taught me the effectiveness/ forcefulness of writing simply, without frills. Even the simplest word can be a source of inexhaustible thought.

I felt honoured when Pascale Mussard, beloved friend of Jicky since childhood, rushed to Sirolo as soon as she was informed about the ceremony for the historical plaque affixed to the house where Jicky lived.

Tributes must also go to Dorothy Varty and Anthony Piercey. With Dorothy I often discussed Jicky's activities as a secret agent, which she already knew about. Anthony, meanwhile, was instrumental in discovering how Jicky managed to free herself from the Nazis.

My gratitude to Mario Maggi, my father. He made me realise that history is not only made up of famous people and that it is essential to write about the invisible ones who made history great.

Finally, I would like to thank Heather Williams, Rights Manager and Commissioning Editor of Pen and Sword, who immediately felt the importance of publishing Jicky's life and sacrifice, making an invisible and forgotten woman who made history great known internationally.

Preface

As the years slip by, so do the living memories of those tumultuous and tragic times when Europe was plunged back into another world war. The men and women who fought bravely for their country and survived are dwindling in number, their personal tales to be told no more. Many, of course, have had their deeds and heroism recorded for posterity by historians and archivists, and have been decorated in recognition of their valour, many posthumously.

But this is no such story of celebrated glory. Told for the first time, it is the account of one woman's life that has not been heard before; an English spy in Nazi-occupied Paris who was captured while pregnant and tortured, but survived and continued to help the French Resistance. It is also very much her personal story; those post-war years when she was caught up in the social whirl of the liberated French capital, marrying into one of its famously rich families of fashion, before settling in a corner of Italy. She was born Hazel Smith (becoming Juvénal-Smith after her marriage) to a well-to-do family near London, but to everyone she became known by her *nom de guerre*, Jicky, taken after the Guerlain perfume, renowned, as she was, for daring sophistication.

When German forces occupied Paris in June 1940, Jicky was already in place, working undercover in the British embassy. The ambassador and his staff evacuated the capital, along with thousands of others fleeing the Nazis and joined the retreating British army. But Jicky stayed behind. A month later, at a secret address in London's Baker Street, wartime Prime Minister Winston Churchill ordered the establishment of the Special Operations Executive (SOE), which was to be placed under the Minister of Economic Warfare with the mission to 'set Europe ablaze'.

The SOE was a merger of three existing secret agencies and was tasked with conducting espionage, sabotage and reconnaissance in occupied Europe, and to support the various resistance movements. The SOE's very existence was a secret. It was known to some as 'Churchill's Secret Army', and some of its carefully selected and trained recruits were parachuted behind enemy lines or dropped off by fishing boat. The women of the SOE and the SIS (Secret Intelligence Service), were later hailed, rather romantically, as 'Churchill's Angels'. Their missions were anything but glamorous, however. Of those sent to France, at least fifteen paid the ultimate price and were killed in combat or captured, tortured and executed. Able to blend in and move around, and less likely than men to be rounded up for forced labour, the Angels were a vital component of British intelligence.

Jicky, who had been in Brussels but was already placed in Paris before German forces took over the city, was chosen for intelligence work at the embassy for her social sophistication and language skills – the benefits of a privileged upbringing.

Growing up in the county of Hertfordshire, she had enjoyed the privileged life of a magnificent country house and domestic servants, even including, she recalls, someone responsible for simply polishing the silverware. However, unlike many upper-class women at that time who were generally educated at home, she was given the opportunity to study and specialised in history and languages. Aside from being extremely cultured, however, she was also selected for her unusual talents in psycho-analysis and graphology, the analysis of handwriting to evaluate personality characteristics. One of her professors had been a disciple of Jung and trained her in the techniques of divining truth and lies.

As war broke out, she was in her late twenties and was an attractive woman. She had lived a whirl of engagements and cohabitation. Life was all about passion for her. In everything, both private and professional. In post-war Paris she remained an intelligence asset, confidently moving in the world of high society; her next husband was a scion of the Hermès empire. She was always dressed up: Dior clothes, Hermès bags, Cartier jewellry.

Thirsty for knowledge, at least that is what others thought, she was always surrounded by influential people and built up a collection of books covering history, poetry, ancient architecture and art. A young Bernard Buffet, a French expressionist, was among her artistic friends. She also developed an expertise in international law, while her life revolved around the arts. She later moved to Italy and settled in Marche with an Italian companion, who though considerably younger, died some years before her. During that time, she began trading in antiques and met a young girl, Nicoletta, and started to teach her English.

Over many years Jicky began to share her past, providing some of her secret diaries. She was never acknowledged by the British authorities for her sacrifices and contribution. No medals, nothing.

This is her story.

Guy Dinmore
(Former Rome correspondent for the *Financial Times*)

PART ONE

Portrait of an Invisible Angel Against the Nazis

Chapter 1

Hazel or Jicky?

Hazel Juvénal-Smith was an undercover agent for His Majesty's secret services; a real-life spy. Not like the ones described in those famous tales of espionage, where the plot is sometimes so exaggerated that it loses all credibility. Not even like the ones found in official biographies, often gloomy and sad. She was anything but, both charismatic and intriguing. Hazel Juvénal-Smith is part of the history of MI6.[1]

Everybody called her Jicky. Whether it was a cover name or an affectation/quirk, we do not know. It is not even clear when she started to use this name. She said that she had been given the nickname because of her favourite perfume, Jicky, by Guerlain, from the historic French perfume/fashion house established in Paris in 1860. It was one of Guerlain's classic oriental perfumes, strong but also sensual, with the mingled scents of bergamot, lavender, jasmine, amber, sandalwood, vanilla and rose wood. Varied and contrasting tones that suited Jicky's personality well.

Jicky was born in Harpenden, a town in Hertfordshire, 35 miles northwest from London, on 7 November 1913 to a well-to-do family. Every time she described it, you could imagine the dynasty immortalised by novels and historical movies, with its carriages and horses. She lived with her family in a magnificent house full of expensive furniture and ornaments, as well as servants, typical at that time for upper-class families. Her family even had a carriage with a coachman to accompany her to school.

Jicky, however, unlike upper-class women at that time who were generally educated at home, was given the opportunity to study. After moving to London with her family, and then to Brussels, she specialised in history, literature and languages, and later studied in a faculty that would serve her well when working as an undercover agent: a course lasting several years in calligraphic/handwriting analysis.

She was a woman with a strong personality, attractive and extremely cultured. Hungry for knowledge and always surrounded by influential people, she collected books on any subject, from history and poetry to ancient architecture and antique furniture.

Such an interesting character could not go unnoticed by His Majesty's government, which took her into its ranks, giving her the role of undercover agent in the secret services. Despite the times, when women were almost always confined to the family and typically female roles, especially amongst the aristocracy and upper classes, the secret services did not want to lose a potentially talented agent. From this point of view, and particularly at that time, they were extremely far-sighted.

During the Second World War, Winston Churchill and his government used many women as secret agents, especially in France, where about sixty were sent. Someone, rather romantically, nicknamed these women 'Churchill's Angels', even though they were very active, risking their lives daily.

The moment when declarations were made by the head of MI6, Alex Younger, was still far in the future. The press agencies reported his appeal on 26 January 2017: 'The real super-expert in technology, whose code-name is "Q" and who supplies hi-tech and lethal gadgets to James Bond, is a woman.' This information was revealed by Younger, who launched a campaign to recruit new agents in the British foreign security services. In the James Bond movies, however, the character has always been played by a man. Younger invited potential female recruits not to have stereotypes about spies, recalling that this type of career is open to everyone, particularly women, upon whom the agency increasingly depends. In May 2025, it was reported that MI6 was ready to appoint its first woman in its 116-year history, with Blaise Metreweli being announced as the new head one month later, on 15 June. Once upon a time, before the war, this would all have been science fiction. After all, the appointment of Stella Rimington as head of MI5 had not happened until 1992.

In 1965, Rimington settled with her husband in India and then joined MI5. Later, when she returned to England in 1968, she was taken on permanently, before becoming the Director General of MI5 in 1992. Afterwards, Rimington wrote spy novels. Her job as an undercover agent with MI5 was in counter-espionage, investigating anti-terrorism. But her greatest difficulty, as she wrote in her books, was to counteract the machismo/chauvinism of her male colleagues, a task that was brilliantly overcome by this hard-headed and tough-minded woman. If Rimington had such problems in these more recent times, just imagine what Jicky had to contend with in the 1940s. Sir Claude Edward Dansey (1876-1947) had been appointed as deputy head of SIS/MI6 after being tasked with setting up his Z network. In her book *MI9*,[2] historian Helen Fry stated that Dansey also made his dislike of employing female agents very clear. From his personal view, 'they simply were not trustworthy'. At that time, however, Churchill demonstrated an uncommon acumen in allowing the employment of women in active roles in the services.

However, even then, the services had already perceived Jicky's talent and unique potential, combined with uncommon intuition and, furthermore, the knowledge of several foreign languages. England has always recruited the brightest minds among its secret agents, especially during the Second World War. The war of spies played a fundamental part in this conflict. These were not just ordinary spies. Among them was a large group of scientists, mathematicians, physicists and luminaries in various disciplines, including Jicky. All were united in an 'army of intellectuals', as Winston Churchill called the services he organised. A real army of intellectuals who made Allied intelligence more modern and professional, but also more imaginative and creative than the service and intelligence agencies of the Axis countries of Germany, Italy and Japan.

Chapter 2

To Paris with Love

It is not clear exactly when Jicky joined MI6. From London she moved to Brussels, and there had her first serious relationship. They may even have lived together. Jicky set aside considerable time in her life for love and relationships: she could not live without them. Hence her whirling round of engagements, one official marriage and cohabitation. Life was passion. In everything. In her private life, she sought the same strong emotions as those in her professional sphere. She was always on the go. She needed those emotions to feel alive. She would constantly fall in love and when that love became routine, she would end the relationship and find another. The rush of adrenalin was crucial for her work, and also fuelled her emotional side, dictating its rhythm. After her first serious relationship in Brussels, Jicky met Charles D. Lieber, an Austrian Pole who had lived in London and subsequently moved to America, and who she considered to be her great love.

Born on 30 January 1921 in The Netherlands, Charles Lieber had been raised in Vienna, Antwerp and Brussels, and had attended Frensham Heights School in Surrey, England. Charles was a student at the Université Libre de Bruxelles when the Nazis invaded Belgium in May 1940, and because his family was Jewish, he was then obliged to flee via France and Spain to Morocco, before arriving in New York in mid-1941. Charles would go on to serve in the US army from 1942 to 1946, finishing as a second lieutenant. Sadly, his mother would be deported from France to Auschwitz in 1942, while his father and stepmother would spend the war in Mozambique. Charles then worked at Knopf Publishing and headed the college department at Random House until

1964, when he bought academic textbook publisher Atherton Press, later merging it to form Aldine Atherton. In 1980, he acquired Hebrew Publishing Company, the oldest American publisher of Judaica.

Even though Jicky and Charles later followed different paths, they remained in contact to the end of their days via telephone calls and romantic notes, with Charles always sending Jicky red roses for her birthday from the US.

From Brussels, Jicky moved to Paris, at the time of General de Gaulle, in that turbulent period immediately before the outbreak of the Second World War. Here she undoubtedly worked as an agent for the British government, working under cover at the British embassy in Paris. She was a spook, the term used today in MI6 to define those undercover agents hidden in embassies and consulates. She never appeared in official lists. In other words, she was a ghost. Intelligence activity took place even then in the corridors of embassies and ministries and was based on contacts and interpersonal relationships. These unlisted spies were part of an extremely valuable, clandestine structure.

When her relationship with Charles ended, she met a man working for the French Resistance with whom she lived in Paris.

Jicky played an important role in the intelligence community. Among her tasks, she had to decipher the personality of subjects who were spied on by means of calligraphic analysis and report her results to the police. Today, the most advanced techniques of cyberspionage and electronic warfare use electromagnetic waves, the internet, microspies and drones to obtain information on the people being controlled, whereas at that time, handwriting analysis was used and homing pigeons were sent to deliver the most sensitive information. These pigeons, which were widely used by the army in both the First and Second World Wars, were the most rapid means of communication available. They were very reliable in delivering strategic messages written on lightweight paper or microfilm and then put into little tubes attached to the bird's leg.

Homing pigeons are equipped with a kind of internal compass that senses the earth's magnetic field. They have a system orientation based on the position of the sun and an enormous ability to identify visual features of the landscape they fly over.[3]

The story of Paddy, the hero messenger pigeon who was awarded a medal of honour, the Dickin Medal, during the Second World War, is well known. Paddy, who served with the RAF during the Normandy operations in June 1944, was the fastest pigeon to reach England with a coded message from the battle-front beaches of Normandy. The brave bird brought back vital information about the Allies' progress, flying 230 miles in four hours and fifty minutes – the fastest time of any of the messenger pigeons involved in the mission.

In the face of poor weather conditions and the threat of German falcons deployed to intercept Paddy and his comrades, he delivered his message to his home loft at RAF Hurn, containing vital information about the Allied forces' progress in battle.[4] Paddy's record has remained unbeaten, etched in history as the fastest time of any carrier pigeon on a mission: 56 miles (90 kilometres) per hour. The carrier pigeons were trained at RAF Hurn, the British airfield for military service, in Hampshire. The use of carrier pigeons for military operations played a greater role than one might think. The British government still has documents that remain top secret. Only in 1999 were some of these made public by the government itself.

Suffice it to say that, during the Second World War, the Nazis immediately arrested and shot those found in possession of enemy pigeons, even though they themselves made extensive use of this method of communication.

Even towards the end of her life, Jicky was very familiar with the use of carrier pigeons and the current international regulations for their protection. She was highly specialised in communication by carrier pigeons, the section known as MI14.

There has been a revival in recent years of the use of carrier pigeons to send sensitive data. Pigeons can fly without problems even in remote areas, and in the event of a computer blackout due to a Fukushima-type nuclear disaster, or the start of an international war (it is scary to call it the Third World War), carrier pigeons would be the only ones capable of soaring through the air to reveal essential information, according to tests carried out in Britain, which flew pigeons past an atomic source on a boat that emitted a radioactive plume. They are also harder to intercept than messages sent via computers. All modern technologies can be picked up. Messages from carrier pigeons, on the other hand, can only be picked up if the birds are brought down by hawks or shotguns. Carrier pigeons, if captured, guarantee absolute silence and the message they carry is difficult to decipher.

In her old age, when Jicky spotted a homing pigeon near her home in Sirolo in the Marche region of Italy, she was quick to call the Carabinieri to request their immediate assistance, as required by international law, even though the animal was missing the red capsule tied to its leg. As was her duty, she treated pigeons with great respect, as if they were real people.

Chapter 3

Write a Few Lines by Hand...

Jicky's greatest skill was in capturing a person's personality, weaknesses and mysteries with the simple analysis of their handwriting, their calligraphic expertise. For her, it was infallible. An exact science and not pseudoscience as many consider it. 'Handwriting is as unique to each individual as fingerprints,' she said. 'It connotes their psychological and physical particularities.'

Through writing she could reveal many secrets, whether a person was swayed or determined, whether healthy or sick, sincere or false. It was a very powerful weapon in the hands of the secret services who, in this way, were able to control or understand the minds of those they were spying on. Jicky was never wrong in her diagnosis. Nor did she share with anyone the methods and techniques she used to decipher handwriting.

Even later, with friends, when, curious, they flooded her with questions, she would simply make the usual request: 'Write a few lines by hand on a piece of paper and I will know everything about you.' She would then hand over the page, as smug as a lion that has just gored a gazelle. Next, she would quickly hide it under a book or inside a drawer, almost as if to protect it from intruders, and the response would only come after a few days. Not right away.

When one returned to her to listen to the oracle, she would stare at her subject. Examining them with her witty eyes, hidden by the mass of blond hair, she scrutinised them until she could read their soul. That penetrating gaze made them helpless, until she was about to deliver her verdict. She pronounced it in a firm and determined tone and no objections were contemplated. It was as she said and that was that. And indeed, at the end of the day, she was always right.

If you had previously revealed to her that this period was not particularly propitious because of certain ailments, she would dismiss you by telling you that this was not the case and that, on the contrary, you enjoyed excellent health. To a young man who, via a friend, who had begged to have his handwriting analysed by her, she would say that he was weak and that, at 25, he was still being influenced by his mother. She would say this even not knowing the individual personally, all from a simple handwriting analysis. And knowing the person, one could only agree with her: throughout his life, when all was said and done, the person in question had been controlled by his family in all his choices.

In later life, Jicky was handed a card with the handwriting of a well-known politician, Umberto Bossi, who had suffered a serious illness a few years earlier, in 2004. She immediately thundered: 'He is very strong, he will recover, he is very strong, you must not fear!'

If you asked her insistently how she did it, she remained vague, gave no explanation and did not reveal to anyone the criteria she used.

Only in recent years, several scientific studies have attached importance to handwriting expertise in understanding an individual. Experts, just as Jicky said long ago, now claim that handwriting, in addition to revealing an individual's personal traits, can also manifest traces and information about his or her physical health.

Contemporary researchers report in various specialist journals that small details in the way one writes can reveal a number of ailments such as high blood pressure, schizophrenia and even Parkinson's disease. According to scholars, calligraphic analysis manifests more than 5,000 personality traits from the size and shape of the letters, as well as the space between words. A guide with this research was produced by the National Pen Company. It evaluated handwriting pressure from darker to lighter handwriting that signals high blood pressure.

In a patient with Alzheimer's disease, mental faculties are impaired and so, consequently, letters will be irregular or shaky, a sign of the disorder, and writing is slowed down. If the letters in the same sentence slant in different directions, this could reveal the symptom of schizophrenia. Parkinson's disease is revealed by the small size of the letters. The sufferer will write so small that he will not be able to re-read his handwriting afterwards.

Writing demonstrates a subject's energy levels, based on how hard he or she presses the pen to the paper, whether it can be discerned and also whether it shows on the back of the page. Tired people with little energy will write with light pressure. Among other rules, leaving large spaces between words means that the subject loves freedom, while shortened spaces, on the other hand, mean they hate loneliness.

According to the American Handwriting Association, handwriting also demonstrates relational compatibility, personal selection, self-awareness and psychological profile. Currently, scientists believe in the possibility of detecting neuromuscular co-ordination disorders with handwriting, because writing is a message that starts in the brain, as a nerve impulse, which is then transferred to the arm.

They treat the subject as a recent discovery. As a pure innovation. Even though these were theories already held by Jicky many years earlier, which had already been the result of other research. In fact, the field had been extensively studied by renowned analysts and scholars almost a century earlier.

For example, handwriting experts were instrumental in the Dreyfus Affair in 1895 in France. The expert of the Bank of France, Alfred Gobert, was summoned to examine whether the dispatches used to indict Captain Dreyfus for high treason had been written by him. Unfortunately, even before the graphologist's verdict, the decision had already been taken to arrest the captain. After a long period of imprisonment, Commander Picquart set up his own investigative commission, after he had long been suspicious of Commander Esterhazy, a colleague of Dreyfus', due to his acquaintances at the German embassy in Paris. Picquart asked for a sample of Esterhazy's handwriting but he was not believed at first, and his request was not granted. He did not give up, however, and in time managed to prove that the famous cables had been written by Esterhazy. He was the traitor, not Dreyfus. The graphical experts were instrumental in Dreyfus' release from prison, while Esterhazy's handwriting – they claimed – was identical to that of the incriminating sheets of paper.[5]

On the other hand, detractors of graphology consider it pseudoscience due to doubts about its accuracy in identifying mental and physical problems. Despite some criticism, however, nowadays more and more companies are hiring handwriting experts based on the applicant's handwriting reports, and courts are requesting them in court cases, asking for a graphic essay to check the authenticity of a signature on a document. The counsellor invites the examinee to write by dictating sentences, such as 'my name is...', 'I was born on...', apparently banal lines, without meaning, then makes the person sign several times in succession. Next, the person is asked to rewrite the same things in a slower manner, to slow down the signing, and to repeat this two or three times. After an average of three standard A4-sized sheets, the subject is finally observed writing a number in figures and then signing with the hand opposite to the one normally used. This is typically the development of the graphic essay, all strictly with biros and paper, to be viewed by the advisor.

Today, studies show that those who prefer to write by hand, instead of using computers, will find themselves with a better memory, sharper critical capacity and greater conceptual understanding. Now more than ever, people are returning to handwriting, even though an increasing number of young people are no longer able to write because of computers and smartphones. Examiners in competitive examinations and various employers are increasingly demanding rigorously handwritten tests and résumés, so as to be able to determine the personality of the writer. Many teachers also demand handwritten assignments. All this contributes to a revival of handwriting skills.

Graphical investigation can link an anonymous manuscript or even graffiti on the walls to its author, despite attempts to disguise or alter the handwriting itself. It is also effective in cases of forged signatures. The forensic discipline is based on studying both the general characteristics of handwriting – rhythm, pressure, curvature, spatial proportions, speed, rhythmic/arrhythmic inconsistencies etc. – as well as the detailed, structural nuances, consistent gestures, simplifications, complications, and personalised dynamics. This field is expanding, especially with the growing use of biometric signatures on digital tablets. A biometric signature is not simply a scanned version of a handwritten signature. It captures a graphic trace transformed into a secure numerical dataset and records measurable characteristics such as speed, pressure, acceleration and movement through electronic sensors.

The script from which all italics in the West originated is chancery or Italic cursive, a term retained for cursive in computers. It was one of the great contributions of the Italian Renaissance to European civilisation. The first printed text for learning italic was composed by Ludovico degli Arrighi from Vicenza in 1522, the so-called *Manuale dell'Arrighi*.

A modern treatise on calligraphy, *Italico per Italiani*,[6] was written by the Englishman Eric Hebborn, who is more generally known for the forgeries he produced (including, famously, the copies passed off as real ones at the National Gallery in London). He was also a painter, writer and art critic, according to whom: 'The pleasure of writing with beautiful handwriting is the same as drawing: when you learn to do it well, you have the satisfaction of creating a work of art.'

In 2019, the National Pen Company analysed President Donald Trump's handwriting. Despite his fondness for tweets, the president showed papers written in his own handwriting, offering a unique opportunity for analysts. They inferred that Trump does not like to be alone, that he has very high energy spikes and that lines that end in a pointed manner reveal traits of aggression.

The theories described above corroborate what Jicky had argued with conviction many years before, at the time of the Second World War, and show how avant-garde she was. And with her, how modern and open to innovations MI6 had already proved to be at that time.

Even then, the secret service, under Churchill's leadership, used such research methods, proving to be light years ahead. Jicky certainly did not improvise anything. And nothing was left to chance.

From her CV printed in *Fountain Pens: History and Design* by Giorgio Dragoni and Giuseppe Fichera,[7] with whom Jicky had collaborated, we learn: 'Hazel Juvénal-Smith, an expert in antiques and archaeology, was a student of Ania Teillard and a connoisseur of C.G. Jung. A graduate, she is a member of the *Société de Graphologie Française* and the A.I.T.I., (Italian Association of Interpreters and Translators).' Jicky was very proud to have co-authored the book and for her CV to be listed alongside those of the other authors. She displayed it smugly, highlighting with close friends the part about her qualifications.

The famous Professor Ania Teillard (1889-1978) was her teacher. Teillard, a student of Jung and Klages, was an important German psychotherapist and graphologist, who had the intuition and merit of integrating the two disciplines. She renewed traditional graphology by combining it with psychology. Franca Mühlmann described Teillard's approach in the introduction to her book, *The Soul and Writing*: 'Depth psychology and graphology are in fact, for Teillard, interpenetrating territories, and writing is the illustration of an inner landscape where symbols are the means by which the unconscious enters the sphere of consciousness.'[8]

Teillard was a very influential figure in her field, perceiving how psychology could be applied to graphology. In addition to being a student of both Jung and Klages, she collaborated with Pulver, Crépieux-Jamin and Saudek, and was the pioneer of the correspondence between Jungian typology and graphology.

According to Teillard, the soul of an individual can be revealed from their handwriting. In her book, *The Soul and Writing*, she highlights the importance of the relationship between the individual and the collective psyche. She analyses writing through the four Jungian psychic functions that are: intuition, sensation, thought and feeling. According to her, the typology of the introvert and extrovert is expressed through handwriting. She also examines the movements of the libido, understood as the totality of the individual's energy, which she believes can only be understood through two research methods: psychoanalysis and graphology.

As stated by Teillard: 'The whole dynamism of writing depends on the intensity of the libido that is expressed mainly in the intensity of the pressure of the pen on the paper and the combination of other graphological signs.'

She then analysed the four developmental stages discovered by Freud, to show that a subject can sometimes remain at one of these stages of childhood development and, with handwriting, find the traits that characterise these aspects.

Ania Teillard's studies are very important when understanding Jicky's background as a disciple of world-renowned innovative scientists, which was not based on a simple empirical and intuitive approach. They also show that revelations trumpeted in the media in recent years as major innovations are nothing more than a return to discoveries made long ago.

Chapter 4

Churchill and the Secret Service

With the Nazi occupation of Paris, the British embassy closed in May 1940 and the staff on duty were immediately evacuated and repatriated to England. This was not the case for Jicky, who remained in Paris along with many other agents, and certainly with the agreement and the protection of the British government.

Churchill was an ardent supporter of the use of secret services and was very aware of new technologies and codes they employed. 'Set Europe ablaze', by sabotage, Churchill ordered in July 1940, while authorising the creation of the Special Operations Executive (SOE). The SOE was one of the most innovative creations Britain maintained during the Second World War. Its task was to physically sabotage, subvert and resist Nazi diktats in occupied Europe, whereas SIS (Secret Intelligence Service) agents overseas were more involved in intelligence gathering.

The British SIS officers worked at embassies and consulates, collecting and analysing military, economic and political intelligence to prepare reports for the Foreign Office. This intelligence was to guide the government and, in times of war, the War Office. Some agents were dropped by parachute or carried by speedboat, even by submarine.

The SOE often recruited personnel skilled in radio transmissions and telegraphy to enable communication between the British government and Resistance movements, thereby supporting the conventional Allied forces with so-called 'secret weapons'. Personnel received rigorous training in Morse code, wireless telegraphy, codes and cyphers, map reading, orienteering, outdoor survival, fieldcraft, weapons training, explosives and demolitions training, silent killing, parachute jumping and how to live clandestinely in enemy-occupied territory.

Acclaimed for their activities at Bletchley Park, the agents provided secure information to the head of their country section, who forwarded relevant parts to intelligence officers in the Army, Navy or Air Force, with a copy to the War Office. 'The SOE was not the only agency to have enlisted female agents,' writes Bernard O'Connor in his book *Churchill's Angels*. 'It is also possible that a number was sent out by SIS, OSS or other agencies.'[9]

It is not known by whom Jicky was sent. With her characteristic reserve, she never mentioned it. Like many others, she spoke French well and arrived in Paris from Brussels. Nor are there any traces in her diaries found later. She is not supposed to have been on official lists, but simply operational and hidden in the British embassy in Paris in that tumultuous period before the outbreak of the Second World War.[10]

After 1940, when diplomatic staff were evacuated from British embassies and consulates in enemy-occupied countries, she was kept in Paris as a secret agent clandestinely. Otherwise, the British government would have awarded her some official honour or recognition, which she never received. Or else her name was absent-mindedly forgotten in some dusty file cabinet due to some oversight.

Among the tasks of the intelligence services was to gather confidential information by identifying the sources, usually those people who had access to state secrets. They then had to analyse their character traits, whether they were strong or malleable, and, if considered weak, try to induce them to betray their sensitive information, sometimes simply by promising financial or other incentives.

It is in this specific area that Jicky operated. She put her ability to analyse handwriting at the disposal of the British government to identify the typeface of a person who held state secrets. Or to identify those individuals deemed trustworthy who could later be used by the British. And it was these activities that were carried out covertly by undercover agents in consulates or embassies.

Jicky did not have paramilitary tasks such as jumping with a parachute or using a weapon. She performed functions of an intellectual and psychological nature as one of Churchill's famous 'army of intellectuals'; an equally important and delicate role. It was a conceptual job in addition to the task of organising resistance groups against the Nazis.

According to Terry Crowdy's book, *SOE: Churchill's Secret Agents*,[11] at the end of October 1944 the SOE reached its peak with an effective staff of about 13,000 on the books. Of these, roughly a fifth had the rank of officer and the majority, 9,000, were drawn from the armed forces. Three thousand two hundred were women, 400 of whom had the rank of officer.

Officially, many SOE women served in the First Aid Nursing Yeomanry (FANY), the women's branch of the British army. These women held many roles in the British armed forces, such as driver, hospital employee and clerical staff. It was also a useful organisation where SOE officers could operate, as they were precluded from any regular military service, which was otherwise forbidden to women.[12, 13]

It was Churchill himself who decided to deploy female agents from the very beginning. He was the originator, especially in Nazi-occupied Western Europe. He firmly believed in the potential of women, showing an open-mindedness and modernity that stood out in this historical period. He sent them to Poland, Holland, Belgium (Jicky arrived from Brussels), Yugoslavia and, above all, France. The latter was a crucial hub because it was close to Britain for RAF planes to land.

These women, most of them young, some middle-aged, were perfect for espionage assignments. They were often good-looking, cheerful, well-dressed and glamourous. They were enlisted because they knew several languages, specialised in a specific field, like Jicky, and sometimes received paramilitary training. Many of them were infiltrated into occupied countries, dropped with parachutes from RAF planes. Like angels, they often arrived from the sky. They were aware that their ability to survive was very poor, many of them lasting a maximum of three weeks, or they were caught immediately after landing.

The women did not enjoy the protection of the Geneva Convention. In 1925, amendments were tabled to regulate the treatment of prisoners of war, whereby soldiers captured in war were granted some protection. Intelligence officers, on the other hand, acted undercover and were therefore considered outlawed combatants. If captured, they were given extremely cruel treatment such as torture (physical and psychological), the most ruthless imprisonment and, ultimately, capital punishment.

Despite everything, these valiant women remained convinced of their mission and did not back down. Moved by the love of serving their country and their anti-fascist and anti-Nazi beliefs, they maintained their determination to the point of their own sacrifice, necessary for the good of humanity. According to Churchill: 'Courage is the first of human qualities, because it is the quality which guarantees all others.' The courage shown by these female agents was enormous.

If depression set in, there was always someone from the entourage ready to lift their spirits by improvising some little party. Of course they were all afraid of dying, of the sacrifices and the possibility of being captured and tortured by the Nazis. Their deaths, however, would have served a greater good. They would then serve as an example to other colleagues, a reminder to go on, to fear nothing and to hope. They were true heroines, without aspiring to be.

The Nazis did not give anyone a break. Even women, who, once captured by the Gestapo, were tortured and often murdered. The female agents were interrogated at the Gestapo headquarters in Paris on Avenue Foch, where German counter-espionage also operated from. The buildings, located at numbers 82, 84 and 86, had been requisitioned by the Germans at the time of the occupation of France and were located in one of the most beautiful residential areas of Paris, in the historic centre, not far from the Arc de Triomphe.

In Rome, however, interrogations and torture initially took place in the basement of Villa Wolkonsky, the current residence of the British ambassador, and then the German ambassador's residence in Italy. During the war, the Germans moved their activities to the buildings in Via Tasso, at numbers 145 and 155, which unfortunately became famous during the occupation as a place of confinement and torture by the Schutzstaffel (SS), the Nazi Party's paramilitary security service, of 2,000 anti-fascist prisoners.

In Paris, right on Avenue Foch, foreign secret agents were interrogated and imprisoned. Many female agents were then transferred to the Fresnes prison outside Paris, others to labour camps. Many women were sent to the concentration camp at Ravensbrück, 90 kilometres from Berlin. Founded in 1939, it immediately became notorious for the torture inflicted on female prisoners. Women were beaten, hung or shot. Many died of malnutrition, others of cold, as they had to endure the freezing German winters with little clothing. Medical experiments were also performed on them. Once the position of foreign secret agent was established, following the violent interrogations, beatings and torture in the labour camps, they were classified as *Nacht und Nebel* (N-N), 'night and fog' prisoners, the name given to the most dangerous prisoners, the political ones.

The *Nacht und Nebel* inmates, both female and male officers, were treated in the worst manner and with the least restraint. They wore the two 'Ns' for Nacht and Nebel written on their backs. Just like the night and fog, they had to be disappeared. To remain invisible. That was the meaning. In time, after receiving the cruellest of treatments, they were killed by execution, if lucky. Others were killed in the gas chambers and their bodies burnt in a crematorium.

First, however, they were subjected to all kinds of torture, always indoors in solitary confinement, in the dark, with their hands and feet bound in chains. In these conditions, they could neither wash nor feed themselves without the use of their hands.

Food and water rations were kept to a minimum. At night they were often beaten and tortured. The lucky ones managed to die immediately from the hardship. Others, however, remained in these conditions for a long time, indoors, alone, always with their hands and feet tied. Beaten repeatedly, in cycles, until the final execution. No traces were to remain of them, nor were they ever to be named again. Night and fog would make them disappear forever, shrouded in an eternal blanket.

One of Britain's bravest and most famous officers, detained in another concentration camp under the classification *Nacht und Nebel*, was the Indian princess Noor Inayat Khan, who, given the codename Madeleine, was one of female wireless operators parachuted into France. Caught following a tip off from an acquaintance, she was interrogated at length by the Gestapo and taken first to prison in Pforzheim and later to the extermination camp in Dachau. Considered by the Nazis to be a very dangerous prisoner, an 'N-N', she was executed via a gunshot to the back of the head after a long ordeal. Based on the testimony of other inmates, the writer Robyn Walker reported that Noor had remained in solitary confinement for ten months, her hands and feet shackled. The chains prevented her from eating, drinking and washing.

She was often beaten, especially at night. She was never taken out into the open air. On 11 September 1944, the Gestapo took her from the prison in Pforzheim and, together with three other prisoners who were imprisoned in Karlsruhe, she was taken to the Dachau camp. Other Dachau prisoners later testified that Noor was beaten and tortured on the night of 12-13 September. After her death, her valour was recognised with the French Croix de guerre decoration and the British George Cross. Noor was part of the SOE's official lists, which is why both countries gave her due honour.

Noor, like so many other agents, despite their unquestioned ability, was discovered because the cunning Nazi death machine had devised an attractive method of catching foreign spies. It offered money to those French citizens who reported their presence. With this system many male and female agents were caught, betrayed by unsuspected people, or by some harmless neighbour or even by friends. Before being sent on a mission, agents were offered an 'L' pill, a rubber-coated capsule containing potassium cyanide. Hidden in a hole specially drilled by a dentist in one of their wisdom teeth, the agent could extract it with their tongue and bite it. Swallowing the poison, they would be dead in fifteen seconds. O'Connor's research showed only one female agent, Hilde Meisel, committed suicide.

On 17 April 1945, on her way back to Switzerland, Meisel ran into an SS patrol in Feldkirch, which was on the lookout for illegal border crossings. An expert marksman shot her through both legs as she tried to escape. Bleeding profusely, she managed to bite hard on her 'L' pill before the SS guards could reach her. A memorial plaque to Hilde Meisel can be seen at Landhausstrasse 3, Berlin Charlottenburg, where she lived for a time.[14]

Most women felt they had to endure torture as there were many people who depended upon them. The SOE's instructions to agents was to withstand the torture for at least twenty-four hours to give their colleagues in the Resistance a chance to excape. The best method of enduring torture was to count – and keep counting. After a day's torture they could continue to keep quiet or tell the Germans some of the truth. Some gave the Germans what they wanted to know, and were subsequently killed.

To spare agents the guilt of suicide by cyanide, they were told that the Catholic Church would give them a special dispensation, absolving them of the sin in the case of suicide. This, of course, was also extended to male colleagues. Some sought a priest to hear their confessions before each mission, fearing they would never return home. Jicky, however, never made a secret of it; she was not a practising Catholic and did not go to church.

Once captured, an agent's cooperation was initially requested but once their absolute refusal was established, they were all tortured. It is unnecessary to dwell on the torture inflicted during interrogations, which ranged from beatings to the extraction of teeth or fingernails from hands and feet and the breaking of upper and lower limbs. Often the torturing executioners came from the same country as the victim. A devious trick devised by the Nazis to publicly conceal their guilt in the barbaric massacres.

During training, agents were instructed on how best to lie during an interrogation by the Nazis. Skill in telling lies could save their lives. They had to remain calm and look the interrogating officer in the eye, in a very natural way, without betraying their emotions or revealing the secrets of their mission. With great courage, they had to resist and not reveal military information, details of SIS or SOE staff, training schools, other agents or contacts with members of the Resistance and details of the mission to which they had been assigned. Also to be avoided were any gestures that could signal nervousness or stress, such as repeatedly touching one's hair. Body language could hide insecurity. During training, they would practise being interrogated by superiors of the British services, with the same vehemence simulated. Other training included being able to sense if someone was tailing them and, if so, how to evade capture. If they noticed they were often being followed, they had to change their home address immediately. Also crucial was the ability to change one's personality, dominating and hiding the real one, to a new one. It was all about invention and cover-up. In short, they had to have two faces.

In their favour, however, was the fact that at first, the Nazis did not realise that these cheerful and lively girls might actually be highly skilled agents of His Majesty's services. Winston Churchill was well aware of this and managed to fool everyone. And this was despite the fact that one of the most famous spies, the Dutch dancer Mata Hari (real name Margaretha Geertruida Zelle), a double agent, was hired by the German consul Alfred von Kremer in the service of Germany during the First World War.

Mata Hari had been an unusual case. Essentially an artist, charismatic and seductive, she had no adequate training in espionage. Once her collateral activities were discovered, she was executed by capital punishment. Nothing to do with the paramilitary organisation of female intelligence network conceived by Winston Churchill. A capillary structure with hierarchical organisation, co-ordinated by the British government of female spies extremely well-trained in their tasks.

During Second World War, the Germans did not realise at first that the women were being used in this manner. In the Nazi imagination, a woman was typically relegated to domestic roles, except for the occasional wife of a few Nazi hierarchs who helped with her husband's activities. And for Eva Braun. Hitler, it was said, never wanted children. He considered himself a genius and therefore none of his descendants could have matched his level of intelligence. For the Nazis, the role of women was summed up by the slogan of the three Ks: *Kinder, Küche, Kirche* (children, kitchen, church).[15] The good Nazi housewife received honours if she bore many children.

The Nazis did not understand, at first, the British government's use of women in the most sensitive intelligence roles. Yet the women also had other potentials. They could conceal ammunition in handbags or bicycle baskets (although the Geneva Convention forbade women from carrying arms, Churchill authorised this anyway), as well as hiding messages to be delivered. They passed unnoticed by the Nazi checkpoints, walked casually around the markets, shopped in the stores. They were thus able to check and view all kinds of information undisturbed. Many women, especially in France, helped the RAF anti-aircraft by providing intelligence. Those pilots returning from a mission in Germany, their engines failing and landing in France, were hidden and, often if wounded, even treated by British agents who also brought them food or medicine in the various basements, attics, or cupboards under the shops where they were secretly housed. They were then helped back to England to prepare for new air missions. Pro-Allied resistance members also helped downed RAF pilots to escape over the Pyrenees.

One of the female agents' tasks was to provide information on the number of German soldiers used in the various districts or checkpoints. The girls would pass by, pretending to be naive, then actually keep track of how many soldiers were at a particular post. They would then identify the locations and type of production of the German military factories, which was essential information for Allied air raids.

We do not know the exact rules of engagement undertaken by Jicky, who certainly did not limit herself to espionage tasks from a secret office, but was very much active in the field. She travelled, met people, exposed herself. One of the tasks of an agent was to aggregate local groups for the Resistance, and Jicky recruited civilian patriots to join these units.

Charles de Gaulle had founded the Resistance organisation the 'Free French Forces' in 1940, with the aim of continuing the fight against the Axis powers. These units were made up of civilians ready to fight the Nazi occupation. Their numbers increased following the German introduction of labour laws. As many German men were needed in the Wehrmacht (Army), Kriegsmarine (Navy) and Luftwaffe (Air Force), there were fewer men available to work in the factories, the mines and the fields. Men in German-occupied countries between the ages of 18 and 40 were required to register to be sent to work in Germany, but instead of forced labour, many men fled and hid in the hills where they were supplied with food, clothing, money, and medicine, as well as weapons, ammunition, explosives and sabotage equipment by the British. SIS and SOE agents worked with them to coordinate their activities in the run up to D-Day.

These men formed armed Resistance groups called *Maquis*, named after the Mediterranean vegetation found on the hills of southern France. The Maquis was the French national Resistance and liberation movement during the Second World War and its partisan members were called *maquisards*. A resistance structure had been created in the territory made up of partisans and people. Their mission was not only one of insurrection and sabotage; they also ensured that the population was cared for, they looked after the needy, and searched for medicines and foodstuffs. Those who had medical knowledge made themselves available for the care that the state could no longer provide. Everyone was ready to help as much as they could with their own means and specialist skills.

Jicky's French boyfriend was a member of the Resistance. The pair lived together in a very small flat, later bought by her, which was well-located in the centre of the French capital. At night she moved around Paris by bicycle or on foot. The city was silenced by the Nazis, who forbade the use of cars, vans and other mechanised means of transport at night. Having a bicycle thus became a real asset. Jicky managed to go unnoticed despite her constantly well-groomed appearance, her glamorous Parisian touch, rosy lipstick and perfect manicure, sophisticated perfume, pure silk scarf and the latest fashionable hairstyle. She was an ideal woman in the German imagination, who tended to be less suspicious of people from the bourgeois or aristocratic classes.

***

Everything proceeded as normal for Jicky, albeit within the dramatic framework of the war. German troops had marched on France in May 1940, with the rapid speed of the German advance catching the British and French troops unprepared, forcing them to retreat towards the English Channel. The German military attack, which started from the north through Holland and Belgium, had reached France. In less than a month, the Germans had succeeded in crushing the Allied armies towards the French coast at Dunkirk. Most of the British army – and part of the French army – managed to escape and over 330,000 were evacuated to England thanks to Churchill's prompt intervention with his Operation *Dynamo*. By June, the Germans had already reached the outskirts of Paris.

While the Nazis occupied the French capital, Parisians were holed up in their homes. This was the period of the four-year occupation and only General de Gaulle, who operated from London, resisted in France. De Gaulle, who described himself as a 'proponent and theoretician of motorised warfare', was the commander of an armoured division at the end of the French campaign. He moved to England following the Dunkirk retreat and, after the Franco-German armistice in 1940, founded the Free France Resistance movement from there. He became Head of the Provisional Government in Algiers and then President of the French Council, after the Liberation, until January 1946. In 1947 he founded the *Rassemblement du Peuple Français*. After a five-year private retirement from the political scene, he founded the Fifth Republic and became its first president in 1959.

De Gaulle was a key figure in this period of France's history, even if his role has been strongly criticised. On the day the Allies entered Paris with tanks, it was he who delivered the speech at the city hall. Some historians have argued that Churchill did not particularly esteem de Gaulle, regarding the unilateral surrender of France as a betrayal, since the French government had made clear commitments to the British government in the fight against Germany.

France officially requested an armistice with Germany in June 1940, accepting very heavy conditions that, in fact, hit the French population hard. Three fifths of French territory and its ports on the Atlantic fell under Nazi control. The imprisoned French soldiers were to remain prisoners until the end of the war. The defeated French army was demobilised and France was then charged with the occupation costs of the German army. The French territory was thus divided into an Occupied Zone and a Free Zone, the latter also controlled by the Germans, albeit in a less suffocating manner. The Free Zone was called Vichy France because it was governed by this city, even though it always remained a vassal of Hitler. Later, in 1942, to prevent a possible Allied landing in southern France, the Germans also invaded this neutral area, controlled by the Vichy government.

Churchill basically had no propensity for de Gaulle because he considered him too nationalistic. De Gaulle was, however, the one who restored France's greatness. He, too, like Churchill, gave enormous importance to intelligence:

During my inspection, I have at my side General Salan, commander-in-chief and in charge of civil powers. He is, due to his career, very familiar with troops and military services; thanks to his experience and taste, he juggles very well with information services that exploit and interpret news, keep in contact with the adversary, deceive them with false moves, set traps for their leaders as in the days of colonial expeditions.[16]

General de Gaulle did not value the role of women in intelligence as Churchill did. His view of the world and of the female role was conventionally male and chauvinistic. His conception of women was more akin to that of the Nazis. Indeed, de Gaulle awarded honours and commendations to very few women at the end of the Second World War.

Jicky moved and operated in this historical context. She became pregnant with her French partner, continuing to work as an agent even though she was expecting a baby. She carried hope. Then the most painful moment of her existence arrived, the one that would change her forever and make her question everything. As an elderly woman, she would later recount what had happened to her close friends:

> One day we were at home and we heard a knock at the door. We went to open it. It was the Nazis. They were coming in guns blazing. They arrested us. I was pregnant, but they didn't care. They had found out I was a British intelligence agent. I don't know how they found out, most likely a tip-off. I don't know whose. They had spotted us. They were sure of it. They had come to take us. They wanted us. They separated us. They captured me and then took me to prison. The cell was cold, so cold and I was pregnant. They took me by the arm and threw me on the cold floor in the dark. I had nothing to cover myself with. It was icy.

Then she would interrupt the narrative abruptly, her voice controlled at first, breaking, almost desperate. Each time she recounted her arrest, she would freeze at this precise point in the narrative, so detailed was the beginning, so obscure the ending. She would not say what exactly had happened during the interrogation and during her detention in prison. She told what happened before, she told what happened after, but in between was the omission, the mystery, the blank line. She never mentioned what they had done to force her to talk. The emptiness. An emptiness that lasted a lifetime.

She never admitted to being tortured. She never described what happened in those moments exactly, nor how long she was imprisoned. Her child was not born in prison, so she was not held for long. No more than nine months. Her son Claude was born on 20 June 1944 so she was clearly captured either in late 1943 or early 1944. Presumably in the winter between 1943 and 1944, as she always spoke of her cell as a cold place. She was without a bed and chairs and was therefore forced to sleep on the floor without blankets and pillows. In the polar cold.

She somehow managed to free herself, avoid death and not end up in the women's labour camps. This was probably because she was pregnant and the Nazis had not found in her a physique suitable for hard work. Or perhaps they were unable to find any concrete evidence of her guilt and so were forced to let her go free. It is highly likely that she had been helped by Resistance groups.

Jicky never recounted how she got out of prison. Her despair at being interrogated by the Gestapo and her stay in Fresnes prison, together with the trauma she had suffered, had blocked her speech, preventing her from clarifying all the other crucial details of that period. She never even reported the imprisonment of her companion, the father of her son, the Frenchman from de Gaulle's Resistance group. Whether he had also been tortured, during interrogation, and how long was he in prison for was not stated.

Jicky was one of the few agents who survived interrogation and prison, maintaining an heroic silence about military secrets. Not to mention being pregnant at the time as well. Almost all of the other women, after being interrogated and put in prison, were sent to female concentration camps. Testimonies show that some of them, after being stunned by injections given by their Nazi executioners, were sent to the crematoria in a perfectly conscious state, while still awake. They were still fighting against their torturers as they were dragged into the hell ovens and burnt alive.

A few agents miraculously managed to escape from the Nazis. Once free, they were helped to England, crossing the Alps into Switzerland or the Pyrenees into Spain and then Lisbon in Portugal or Gibraltar. Many of them then decided to return to the field as soon as possible to continue the mission they had undertaken, heedless of the dangers they faced. Often, however, the British government preferred not to send them back to enemy-occupied territory as their personal details would have been known and stored in the Gestapo archives. Only a couple of cases of betrayal of British agents by the Nazi enemy are recorded. They were promptly captured by the British government at the end of the war and imprisoned for many years in prisons in England.

Once Jicky was released from prison, she stayed hidden in France, helped by a few colleagues from the British intelligence and French Resistance groups. She gave birth in 1944 and weaned her son. On 6 June 1944, the Allied troops landed at Normandy, the beginning of the end of a nightmare and the birth of a new period in history. The Liberation.

***

Often over the years, Jicky would repeat the story of her arrest, almost as if to exorcise it and show herself and others that she had made it, she had overcome it. Omitting the real reasons, i.e. that she was an agent of the British intelligence, she would tell the story of the Gestapo to anyone who visited her. Her resistance as an example to those who told her of their daily difficulties. If *she* had made it out of Hell, everyone could face all kinds of tribulations.

Surely, in that emptiness, there had been so much pain. When she interrupted the reenactment of that time, she always remained silent with a pensive gaze, lost in the emptiness of her world. Always the same distraught attitude, her eyes glassy.

Although she gave nothing away about being tortured by the Gestapo, it is known that the Germans tortured all British agents they discovered. One can clearly guess, therefore, that she had been too.

In the last months of her long life, when the nurse would go to her house to nurse her and stick the needle into the vein battered by too many intravenous jabs in her arm, Jicky would sometimes, in a state of semi-consciousness, shout at her in annoyance: 'You Nazi!'

Chapter 5

The Hermès Family

Hell had ended on Liberation Day. The Allied tanks entered Paris on 25 August 1944, bringing with them so much hope. The horror was over: life was returning. De Gaulle gave a glimpse of the future, gave his nation the chance to believe in a better tomorrow, in the greatness of France.

Jicky gave birth to a beautiful child, Claude, in June 1944, the same year of the Liberation. He had the same porcelain complexion as her and was vivacious and witty. After a short time, however, she ended her relationship with the father of her child, the French Resistance fighter. She continued with her job at the embassy, once it reopened, remaining in intelligence. Immediately after the Liberation, she was also active and worked for a strong revival of culture and art. It was during this period that she met and fell in love with Monsieur Jean Juvénal, an elegant and aristocratic man from the Hermès family, the famous and historic French *maison* of fine leather goods known throughout the world.

The Hermès company started business as a horse harness workshop in the Grands Boulevards district of Paris in 1837. It then served the French nobility, producing the finest harnesses and bridles for carriages. Thierry Hermès was its founder and later passed the management of the company on to his son, Charles-Émile Hermès, who moved the shop to where it is today, at 24 Rue du Faubourg Saint-Honoré. It was he who started to produce saddlery and bags, designed especially for horse riders, although it was not until 1920 that a clothing collection was produced, the first item being a golf jacket made for the Prince of Wales. Then in 1922, Charles-Émile Hermès' daughter-in-law complained that there was no handbag on the market that satisfied her refined tastes, and so he designed one especially for her. It was not until the 1930s, however, that the iconic bag, later named Kelly, was conceived. It was thus that the Hermès/Dumas family began their entrepreneurial activity.

Monsieur Juvénal fell head over heels for the proud and charismatic Jicky. A beautiful girl, tall, slender and feminine at the same time, who was very sophisticated and shrouded in an inexplicable aura of mystery. A delicate blonde beauty with a porcelain complexion that contrasted with her enormous determination. Her haughty and confident advance and the power of her gaze were enough to perceive her strength from the first impact. Not to mention her charm and her magnetic, enigmatic eyes. Even their colour. Bluish grey. Or greyish blue. Indefinable. He wooed her insistently with bouquets of flowers and countless love letters with irresistible French gallantry.

He proposed marriage to her and Jicky became Madame Juvénal and entered the wealthy Hermès family. The well-to-do English rose, the typical Anglo-Saxon beauty, entered the world of French high society.

Madame Juvénal began to frequent the jet-set of the time. She attended parties, openings, cultural circles and met many artists and fashion designers. If in Brussels she had met Magritte, in Paris she became friends with Bernard Buffet, an exponent of Expressionism and member of the Anti-Abstract Art Group. Jicky later took Buffet's etchings to all her homes, especially the one in Venice, with a view of the lagoon, where it was hung on the wall in her bedroom.

She met Yves Saint Laurent and his long-time collaborator and partner Pierre Bergé, becoming close friends with both. She shopped in the most famous Parisian boutiques, including Christian Dior. She had an almost liturgical relationship with the old Guerlain shop, where she often went to buy Jicky perfume. She frequently recalled with nostalgia that almost magical boutique in the centre of Paris, with its wooden interior and beautifully displayed bottles.

Jicky loved to describe the Paris of the time. Where well-dressed ladies, wearing hats and gloves, walked arm in arm with gallant men with canes. 'Women loved to dress up,' she often recounted, 'and go to the best hairdressers in Paris, strictly wearing the Kelly, the legendary Hermès bag. They would lay it on the floor absent-mindedly, while having their hair done, reading a good book.' The Kelly was the only bag Jicky would wear, the only one she loved, not just because all she had to do was simply walk into the famous Hermès boutique, choose the model and walk out without paying. For her, the Kelly was so much more. It was beautiful and elegant, and therefore the only bag that could represent her. She was already wearing the Kelly long before Grace Kelly used it to conceal her advanced state of pregnancy, later giving the accessory her maiden name. It could have been called the 'Jicky' of Hermès, were it not that Grace Kelly was the famous Princess of Monaco.

'The handbag for a woman is very important,' Jicky said.

> It contains her life and her mysteries, it gives her a connotation. I remember when I chose mine, not a Kelly already available in the Hermès shop, I had it made especially for me. I chose, from the samples of the various leathers, the shiny brushed calfskin, in dark brown with a very particular shade of black. I then asked the craftsman to create it with a soft, rounded shape, unlike the others which were rigid, and not in the standard size, but longer, suitable for me, who always carries a book and can't go too long without reading. When I picked it up, it was splendid, the most beautiful bag in all of Paris.

The truth is that Jicky loved her bag not just for its luxury and elegance. Many ladies loved to show off, for them the Kelly was, and still is, a status symbol, something to flaunt. Not so for Jicky, who saw in that bag her family, her affections, a container of feelings. It was the product of an entire generation. The house of Hermès. A symbol. While many women put a portrait charm on their chain with a photograph of their loved one or some family member in it, she proudly wore that bag on her arm. It represented the whole world of Hermès, tradition and thus her roots. It was her identity.

Jicky collected everything by Hermès. Dozens and dozens of scarves and, as she would not have the time to wear them all, she had them sewn together, creating beautiful cushions that she or her cats used to sit more comfortably on the sofas in the living room. She had a beautiful rouge Hermès leather case commissioned with different spaces to hold paper, envelopes and stamps. It even had her initials, HJ (Hazel Juvénal), engraved on it: it was a love letter carrier. That is what she called it. A whimsical idea that perfectly represented her innate sense of romance.

She boasted that just two examples of a soft pair of nappa gloves had been reproduced by the Parisian fashion house: one for her, the other for Grace Kelly. She also collected all her notes in small, annual Hermès diaries and kept them all, throughout her years, taking them with her to her home in Sirolo, Marche. There she would write down with a biro, in great detail and tiny script on pale, yellow pages, what she did, what she was supposed to do, how much she had paid for some trips, her expenses, and much more. She transcribed numbers and acronyms that were impossible to decipher, words only she understood. Capital letters next to sets of numbers, then lowercase letters with other numbers next to them. Seemingly meaningless.

In these little books are hidden the many secrets of her life, a unique testament of her experiences. Jicky kept everything like an historical archive, meticulously, as if she wanted to keep her memories in order, in those notebooks, in a box, in the tiny diaries strictly by Hermès. Just as she kept all the letters and photographs of the people she loved most, well separated and catalogued in envelopes or folders.

Her husband had a splendid hotel in Porquerolles, on the largest island of the Hyères archipelago in Provence. The village of Porquerolles, which gives its name to the whole island, is inhabited by about 200 people, but it is tourism that generates revenue and economic well-being. Tourists visit the beaches, go scuba diving, hiking and swimming. It was here in Porquerolles that the Belgian writer Georges Simenon set his detective novel, *My Friend Maigret*, in 1949.

Jicky spent long periods on this magical island with her son Claude. She loved the sea, and the hotel where she stayed was the most beautiful and elegant on the island. Many writers and intellectuals stayed there, and their presence gave her immense pleasure, in addition to the fact that she could admire the natural beauty of the island.

During this period, she slowed down her work at the embassy, staying on the island for long periods while constantly commuting to Paris. The French capital was where she felt the most fulfilled. Her son studied and she had the chance to be more active. She was always involved in the city's artistic and cultural events. After all, too much quiet had always bored Jicky, who had always preferred a dynamic life to the idleness of the high society lady.

***

Jicky had a special relationship with the entire Dumas-Hermès family, Monsieur Pierre Siegrist and his wife, Madame Myriam Guerrand-Hermès. But it was with the little ones especially that she forged a true maternal relationship. In addition to her natural son, Claude, whose intelligence and, later, professional skills as a journalist she continually boasted about, Jicky often spoke fondly of the children of the family, but especially of Pascale Siegrist Mussard (the co-artistic director of Hermès), together with her cousin Pierre-Alexis Dumas, both descendants of Thierry Hermès' family. She considered Pascale's mother, Myriam, almost as a sister.

Jicky doted on Pascale, whom she saw as the daughter she never had. She said of her that she had an innate elegance, simple but very sophisticated. She showed off photographs of Pascale's wedding, radiant with a special hairstyle, a crown made of a simple knotted white cord and a veil. 'A very special bride,' Jicky commented proudly. She often admired the photograph taken on the day Pascale's child was born, with the baby in her arms and her still in bed. And the one with the children lying with Pascale on a colourful beach towel.

She loved Pascale above all because this goddaughter of hers was so tender with her. She called her by the petname *Chère mamaîne* and sent her many letters from all over the world containing family photographs, of her mother, who shared a special bond with Jicky and of her children. Pascale often concluded her letters, written in French, with: 'I think of you very, very often and I embrace you with much, much affection. Pascale.' Jicky was very happy about this.

Years later, when Jicky was already over 90 and living in Sirolo, Pascale phoned her one 7 November to wish her a happy birthday, while she was in the Middle East on business. The proud English lady was so happy that she almost had a heart attack. She struggled to recognise Pascale's voice from how excited she was, almost stammering. She remained so upset that she could not sleep the following night. That phone call to her was a great gift, more precious than any Hermès bag.

Pascale Mussard later recounted anecdotes from her childhood with Jicky. 'My parents made me get up early in the morning, even when I didn't go to school on Sundays or was late at night. Discipline was ironclad. However, when I went to sleep in the big bed with Jicky on Sundays, I could wake up late. She would bring me breakfast to the bedroom on a tray, warm scones she'd freshly baked. For me it was a great joy.'

***

Meanwhile, the splendid aura of Paris increased day by day, becoming more elegant and haughtier. Optimism pervaded among the French as they rediscovered a zest for life and fun. Fairs, circuses and merry-go-rounds were abundant, the birth rate increased and the baby boom began. Fashion and art magically exploded, as did cultural centres and literary cafés. De Gaulle had performed the miracle, resurrecting the capital within a relatively short space of time. France was waking up and returning to its former grandeur.

Jicky's intellectual curiosity was satisfied. Not only because of the kind of cultured people she surrounded herself with, the Olympus of artists, but precisely because, in fact, she never stopped studying. She devoured books of all kinds and was increasingly attracted to history, antiques and art. She cultivated the hobby of cinema and went to see the films of the great French, English and Italian authors. She studied foreign languages. She collected antiques, including an extraordinary series of Victorian inkwells and pens, a multitude of precious glass and ceramic birds, colourful teapots, strange silver and wooden utensils, and books on the most diverse subjects, ranging from texts on the apogee of Queen Victoria to the fairytales of Grimm and Perrault. From the Victorian mansion to Borromini. From antique jewellery to fantastic art, from the birth of London to antique furniture and zodiac signs, with the stars that regulate human behaviour. A volcano of culture and interests, she was always eager for novelty. On the other hand, Jicky had no aptitude for cooking, at least that is what she said, which she considered time wasted taken away from culture, art and travel. After all, she was used to having maids and cleaning ladies at all hours of the day.

When she went shopping, she would go to the shops, choose and pay, without taking the goods home. Instead, the groceries would be delivered to her, as it was not elegant for a lady of high society to be seen with shopping bags in her hands.

Sometimes in summer, when she did not have time for the sea and the beaches of Porquerolles, she would go to the exclusive swimming pool of the Paris Hilton Hotel. It was a dream life, coveted by everyone in the world.

Jicky, however, was beginning to grow impatient. Her perfect marriage to Monsieur Juvénal had turned into a daily routine and was beginning to creak. Romance and love were indispensable to her, like water to a fish. She could not share her life with a man solely out of affection and esteem, and she was certainly not the kind of woman who resigned herself to compromise. Next to a special life in a gilded cage, she preferred oxygen, freedom. After all, she often liked to quote William Shakespeare's phrase: 'The course of true love never did run smooth,'[17] to reassure her friends, but above all her, that the course of true love, to be special, did not have to be easy.

Jicky really did love her husband, she adored him. The counter-evidence was the fact that, in the last years of her life, she sometimes repeated to herself that perhaps she had made a mistake in leaving that solid marriage. She expressed doubts and perplexity. She must have asked herself questions, whether it would have been better to stay in Paris and be a society lady in an historic family, instead of ending her long life in a pleasant village by the Adriatic Sea, perched on the Monte Conero, in Sirolo, surrounded by the affection of a few trusted friends, but with no family member to live with.

This was her reasoning, many years later. But by then she was no longer happy. To those who asked her later why her princely marriage had ended, she replied candidly: 'There was no more passion.' And she certainly could not live with someone just out of respect. Not at her age. Not without adrenalin.

Chapter 6

Dear Paolo

At this point, Jicky's life underwent a real revolution. She no longer played such an active role in the field as a secret agent, having previously slowed down during her marriage. Now she had the opportunity to travel, and one of her favourite destinations was Italy, which attracted her for its history, culture and artistic beauty. She travelled from Paris by train and arrived in Italy with her beautiful, brown leather suitcase with the golden initials HJ, Hazel Juvénal. Her first stop: Rome, where she worked at the UN.

She told of how she rented accommodation in the historical centre of the capital, in a beautiful little square with a splendid fountain in the centre. According to her descriptions, it was most likely the Turtle Fountain in Piazza Mattei; a charming little square in the Jewish Quarter.

Jicky loved walking through the city centre among the ancient streets and majestic buildings. She visited museums, the Colosseum and archaeological excavations. She did not know many people in Rome. From her personal address book, however, some locals emerged, as well as a few English personalities, although it is not known for sure whether she met them at that time or later. Perhaps she met them at the UN offices? She always kept in touch with her wealthy French family, the Hermès, and her son Claude, who decided to stay in Paris for study and professional reasons.

In Rome, she later recounted that she started dating a photographer, although she never spoke of genuinely falling in love or feeling a great attraction for him. Perhaps it was more a momentary reference point, or because he did not want to make a serious commitment. Perhaps he was married or had another affair? Jicky was not too upset, deciding to remain in Rome, but instead continued to travel around the country, especially central Italy, and often visited Milan.

It was on one of these journeys, again by train, that she would meet a special man, Paolo. At the time she was 48 years old, still a very beautiful and charismatic woman, shrouded in something of a mystery. The pair liked each other at first sight. It was true love. Jicky fell completely head over heels. Paolo was neither cultured, handsome nor elegant. He was seventeen years younger than her (this was the age difference Jicky had always declared), and he captured her with the cheerfulness of youth and the simplicity of a provincial boy.

Paolo Paolini worked at *Il Corriere Adriatico*, a local newspaper, whose editorial office is in Ancona, although it is distributed throughout Marche. He was a printer and lived in Sirolo on the Conero Riviera. The place was magical. The Conero Riviera, with the mountain that drops right down to the Adriatic Sea, leaves anyone who visits it breathless. It looks like a giant rock collapsing into the water. For the local old fishermen, Monte Conero exudes positive energy, attracting people and, at the same time, protecting them against malice. For lovers of esotericism, anyone who has been to Monte Conero (from the Greek *kòmaros*, arbutus/strawberry tree) at least once will remain forever bound to it because of the powerful magnetic forces it emanates.

Local legends tell of fairies and witches appearing at night in the various coves near the sea. For the more rational, however, the place is enchanting all year round for its natural beauty. A mountain that, from a distance, from the Numana seafront, with its white cliffs contrasting with the green of the forest, looks like the snout of a lion resting on the sea, as if crouched on its paws.

Monte Conero is tinged with yellow in spring because of the many brooms that cover it. It is also very fragrant because of its lavender fields. Some even tell of hidden military barracks protecting a secret NATO base. The Conero is all of this: beauty, legend and mystery. 'If you are looking for the paradise of the Adriatic in the Marche, the Conero is the one that most resembles it, writes *Lonely Planet*. It describes Conero as having 'a crystal-clear sea, coves of the whitest pebbles and incredibly green cliffs dotted with the purple of lavender and the yellow of broom.' The atmosphere of the place enchanted Jicky forever.

Jicky began a passionate love affair with Paolo and immediately went to Sirolo to meet him. She loved Paolo, but also his background, and turned her life around for him, leaving Paris for good. Later, she would often talk about this overwhelming love, the intimate days and nights spent in her house in Sirolo, the happiness she found there. She sold her small flat in Paris to buy a house in Sirolo, their love nest. She left office, status and wealth to lead a life of utter simplicity with Paolo in a medieval village overlooking the sea. In winter Sirolo is inhabited by just 4,000 souls, but in summer is repopulated by groups of elegant tourists. The English and Germans live in Sirolo and nearby Numana all year round. Directors of large German companies like Philips, as well as famous entrepreneurs, artists like Artias, Picasso's disciple, who resided in a villa in Numana's Taunus village to work in peace, lived there. British painter John Corbidge spent long periods in Sirolo, and Jicky often chatted with him. As Prince Aga Khan's favourite painter, Corbridge was often summoned to his villa in Sardinia to fresco its interior walls.

Jicky was also attracted to the Conero Riviera by the type of people she found there: bohemian and original, similar to those in Porquerolles. Likewise, Sirolo reminded her of Porquerolles. She complained, however, that the residents of certain small towns in the Marche, the natives, were not adequately educated, that they did not read books by important authors and did not speak foreign languages. She, meanwhile, knew French and Italian in addition to English, her mother tongue. Later, she would also study a very complicated language for a westerner: Russian.

Despite some difficulties in fitting in, Jicky was happy with Paolo. He was not wealthy, but in addition to his passion, he offered her romantic boat trips along the riviera, pointing towards the Two Sisters (Due Sorelle) Beach, with the twin sea stacks, while fishing for mussels and sea urchins. There were sunset aperitifs at the central bar in the square and fish barbecues.

At first, the locals greeted Jicky with some mistrust. In 1960s Catholic Italy, Jicky and Paolo's love was taboo. The fashion for toy boys and Macrons did not yet exist, especially in a small town in the province of Ancona. Seventeen years was a big age difference then, especially if it was the woman who was the elder of the pair. In addition, their union was not sealed by marriage; they cohabited more uxorio.

But Jicky was so brazenly elegant, beautiful and haughty, a true lady. In winter she wore beautiful cashmere jumpers ordered directly from England, Burberry mackintoshes, camel coats by Aquascutum, black or blue blazers with glittering gold buttons with heraldic coats of arms. She wore a fox fur coat by Christian Dior, a diamond bracelet by Cartier. All this was always accompanied by a gorgeous Hermès Kelly.

In addition to this, although she had never revealed that she had worked as a secret agent, not even with her closest friends or those who had joined her in her later years, nor with her neighbours, some of the local elders had found out, perhaps through Paolo, who certainly knew about it and had even nicknamed her 'the spy'. This was a somewhat derogatory term for the delicate job that required great skill and that she had held for so many years. Even an elderly local carabinieri marshal was aware of who she really was. Perhaps the carabinieri had received information about it through institutional channels?

Jicky was strong, however, and did not care for the gossip of her fellow villagers. Instead, she devoted herself to furnishing her newly purchased, beautiful house. Her home was in the historic centre of Sirolo, among the narrow lanes of houses built with stones from Monte Conero. It was very old, from the late seventeenth or early eighteenth century. When she showed people around it, she liked to say, proudly, that it was the original home of the town's parish priest, who was very powerful at the time. The church was only a few metres away. Later, the house was used by the bishop of Ancona as a summer holiday residence.

The underground village, dating back to the Middle Ages, is formed by a multitude of tunnels and underground passages, so that from the parish priest's house, one could reach the church and the square. Jicky explained how the steps on the ground floor, near the woodshed, with the subsequently sealed tunnels, were low and wide, designed for the use of horses with their riders. The bathroom was also very old, with stone walls; only the sanitary fittings were modern. Then there was the original staircase, which led to the living floor. If torches had been used instead of rare antique lamps, it could have been perfect for a medieval castle.

On the first floor was a huge hall with original ceilings. The furniture, strictly antique, from the nineteenth century, was mostly from the Marche region, and a few smaller pieces had come from England. Period paintings were hung all over the walls, with the addition of a few precious etchings by Bernard Buffet. On the crystal tables were trinkets from various journeys, special pieces that told the story of a lifetime. There was also Jicky's famous collection of birds, inkwells and Victorian pens. An old bookcase laden with volumes of all kinds, not to mention many photographs with Paolo. From the pictures taken over their many years together, one could clearly perceive how happy they were. Jicky always beaming beside him, almost ecstatic. Pure love in their mature years, when most couples resign themselves to relationships of great affection and esteem and above all to a life of routine. They always had that expression of an eternal honeymoon couple, despite the passing years.

Also on display was the photograph of her son Claude, now divorced, who remained in France after having been a correspondent in many parts of the world as a journalist, and her two grandchildren, a boy and a girl, also in Paris with their father to study.

From the drawing room one could then access two rooms with painted ceilings and very high walls used as guest rooms. In one of the rooms, a fresco depicting the Madonna of Loreto dominated from above. In another, stucco shells protruded from the ceiling, neatly arranged in the corners of the room. In the first, an enormous bookcase in solid wood, possibly walnut, from the early twentieth century stood out, overflowing with her beloved books.

The living room then led to the dining room, her real headquarters. Large, bright with a huge fireplace in the centre, it was the only source of heat in the whole house, since Jicky had refused to have radiators installed so as not to spoil the beauty of the old walls. In winter, if one did not almost embrace the enveloping flame with the warmth emitted by the burning wood, it was easy to freeze in the house. Sirolo is by the sea, but perched on Monte Conero, and among the narrow streets of the village, an icy wind crashes against the outlines of the ancient dwellings in the alleyways, until it penetrates into the bones.

Jicky spent much of her time in the dining room. On the wall were half-point paintings and small oil portraits from her well-to-do English family. Copper vases and plates were neatly displayed on a plate rack. Above a shelf, ceramic teapots, antique cups and silverware, fruit plates, cutlery and trays were on display. In all her life, Jicky said that she had never drunk tea with a spoon that was not made of silver. While the English use the idiomatic expression, 'born with a silver spoon in one's mouth' to define a person who has had a very privileged upbringing or who comes from a wealthy family, in Italian something similar to it would be: *'nato con la camicia'* (born with a shirt), even if in this particular case it is more about being lucky in life. As a matter of fact, Jicky was born with a silver spoon in her mouth and had continued to use it forever. As a true Englishwoman, then, she followed the preparation of tea almost maniacally. The milk had to be poured into the empty cup first. The hot water later. Secret agents sent to operate in Nazi-occupied countries, however, were taught from the outset not to follow these customs with the milk before the hot water. It would have been an unmistakable signal of their British nationality.

Also in the large dining room was a small kitchenette, which was essential, given the little care she devoted to cooking, and a huge white refrigerator, where she could keep her butter and her favourite drink, milk, which she had delivered directly from the grocery shop in the small square. Every time she drank it, often in place of water at lunchtime, she could not help comparing it to English milk, which in her opinion was much better and tastier than Italian milk.

From the dining room window, one could admire the roofs of the old village. It was often open, even in winter during lunchtime, because her beloved pigeons came to visit her daily. She would let them find bread and biscuits on the windowsill, sometimes in a saucer left on the imposing wooden table. They flew into the house without fear, ate the crumbs voraciously and came away satisfied, cackling. The pigeons kept her company, she had even given them nicknames and had always loved them, from her days as an agent in British intelligence, when she had to deal with carrier pigeons. When one day, a neighbour, Palmonella, killed one of the birds for no reason, Jicky became very angry and never spoke to him again. To her, he had become 'awful Palmonella'.

From the living room, a walnut door led to the bedroom with a white sofa bed in the middle and two fine bedside tables on either side. Directly opposite the entrance, a wardrobe, also antique, stood out. Next to the bed was the aforementioned Buffet etching depicting the romantic city of Venice and its lagoon. She often admired the painting, fascinated by the beauty of Venice and the greatness of the painter who had depicted it. 'That painting will go to my son,' she repeated.

Everything was so special and whimsical in that house, every detail meticulously studied. Even the door knocker was unique: the delicate, tapered bronze hand of a noblewoman acting as a pendulum. So elegant with the ring on her left ring finger. It was so beautiful that many a bride and groom, out and about in the town for the ritual photographs with the photographer in search of the most picturesque corners and breathtaking views, would stand right in front of the gateway on their special day to have their photograph taken.

***

During the summer, when Paolo was not working at *Il Corriere Adriatico*, he took Jicky out on a fishing boat he had bought. Like many in the area, he was passionate about the sea and fishing. He often dived with a diving mask and went swimming offshore. Paolo's fellow villagers described him as a *viveur*, a funny, young, big guy who was always ready for a joke. As a hobby, he enjoyed boxing. He had also bought an old Ferrari, second-hand, and together the two went shopping in nearby Civitanova Marche.

When she was alone, Jicky walked down the slopes of Monte Conero to the beach or went for walks with her beloved dogs. These, spoilt like children, were always small, long-haired and named after other Guerlain perfumes. After the classic Jicky, used by her because it was her favourite, all the remaining Guerlain perfumes were chosen as names. Shalimar, Samsara, Mitsouko and so on.

Jicky fitted perfectly into this new reality. She spoke Italian very well and invented a job to keep herself busy, choosing an area in which she was already very knowledgeable. In the nearby tourist resort of Numana, a town practically attached to Sirolo, she bought a commercial premises opposite the largest ice-cream parlour, Morelli, in the small, town square and opened a prestigious antique shop. With her characteristic passion, she filled it with unobtainable pieces, and it soon became a point of reference for lovers of antiques and antique furniture. Next to small tables, frames, beds and chests of Italian origin, there were just as many objects from England. The perfect marriage of English and Italian art. The synthesis of pieces from different eras, the eighteenth, nineteenth and early twentieth centuries could only be found in Numana, in her shop. Here one could also find crystal perfume holders, Victorian-era bone combs and frames from the wealthy residences of decadent noblemen. Every corner was crammed with objects with the smell of a bygone age, and Jicky's sumptuous antique shop was on a par with the prestigious ones in London, Chelsea or on Portobello Road, which is quite something considering Numana's resident population.

Every morning, Jicky headed along the road from Sirolo to Numana, either on foot or in Paolo's car, nicknamed *Paolo de pellicciò* (Fur Coat Paolo) by the villagers. No one was quite sure why, but it was probably because his maternal grandfather, Giacinto Fortipiani, was a boatswain in Genoa and when he went to Sirolo, he wore a coat with a fur collar. It is customary in Sirolo to give people nicknames and so the whole family would be christened *de pellicciò*, all because of a fur coat.

Business was good for Jicky, even though in winter there were much fewer residents. Many of the tourists who came in the summer, wealthy people from northern Italy or foreigners, flocked to her shop all year round when they needed to buy important pieces or simply to browse and check if new objects had arrived. To these must be added all those people from neighbouring towns who, having heard about the owner's business and undisputed skills, would come to Numana for expertise or advice.

'One day,' Jicky later recounted:

A well-dressed young man entered my shop. He started peering everywhere. His eyes suddenly landed on a beautiful solid wooden chest. He wanted it at any cost. He asked me how much it cost, I told him I wanted a million lire. Without hesitation he pulled a chequebook out of his pocket, wrote the requested sum on one of them and signed it. All in a very short time. He made arrangements with me for the collection. In a flash he left and I was stunned, with the cheque in my hand. I looked at it, wondering if it would be covered? I carefully read the young man's name: Diego Della Valle, who could that be? Better go to the bank to see if the cheque was covered. And so, the next day, I went to the bank and received the necessary reassurances.

Jicky often told this amusing anecdote. Mr Diego Della Valle, then virtually unknown, was none other than the Della Valle of the shoe and bag fashion house, Mr Tod's. His world-renowned Tod's/Hogan company from the Marche has accessories worn by the likes of Gianni Agnelli, the famous ankle boot worn casually under dresses, or Lady Diana, whose D-Bag is still a must for any fashionable female. Jicky had questioned a cheque from one of the wealthiest industrialists in the country. Proud because Della Valle had bought one of her pieces of furniture, she often giggled as she recounted the incident.

Despite the fact that her life existed between home and a shop, and only in the summer down on the beach in Sirolo, Jicky went to London about once a month for a few days, claiming to buy new material for the shop. It is not known for sure whether she was definitely finished with the secret service, however. She never talked about it, preferring to remain, as usual, in an aura of mystery. As always in the episodes of her life, she recounted the before, she recounted the after, but left the middle out. It is said that those who enter the secret service, although they can change their position and role, will remain in it forever. With Jicky, we do not know how the secret service dealt with her, and whether or not they gave her special leave when she decided to leave Paris. Did she manage to cut the umbilical cord imposed by the British government for good, or only partially?

Chapter 7

Codes, Acronyms and Numbers

In her personal address book, strictly by Hermès, Jicky jotted down the names and addresses of a few London hotels where she went once a month. As she did in her annual, minute diaries, also by Hermès, she wrote in her usual elegant handwriting, but always so small as to make it difficult to read. She noted down the various names and addresses with a black or blue biro, or with pencil. She did not use the famous green ink in any of her booklets, the colour used by the first director of MI6, Sir Mansfield George Smith-Cumming, codenamed 'C' from the initial of his surname, who eccentrically signed documents in this colour when the service was founded in 1909.

The SIS insignia originally consisted of the C with the image of a brain on the inside and the Latin inscription *Semper Occultus* (Always Secret). The basic purpose of the agency was to gather as much information as possible for the interest of the British government. During the First World War, it devoted itself entirely to military espionage and intelligence, with little success in penetrating German intelligence. By the time of Cumming's death in 1923, MI6 had begun operating with the Foreign Office. In embassies located around the world, a Passport Control Officer was appointed, who in reality was none other than the head of British intelligence in that country.

Sir Hugh 'Quex' Sinclair took over from Cumming and decided to expand the functions of MI6. In 1938 he acquired Bletchley Park and its land for military purposes. The service's main cryptanalysis unit, the Government Code and Cypher School, was installed here. Under the management of Stewart Menzies in 1940, British intelligence succeeded in decrypting the German Enigma code, via Ultra, which was one of their greatest achievements at the time.

During the war, more than 10,000 people worked at Bletchley and its branches. Eighty per cent of the staff were women, with Churchill describing them as: 'The geese that laid the golden eggs and never cackled.' A visit to Bletchley Park by Catherine, Princess of Wales a few years ago revealed that her paternal grandmother had secretly served at the base during the war.

In her old age, Jicky never revealed that she had ever been involved in either cryptography (from the Greek *kruptòs* (hidden) and *gramma* (writing)), or codes. However, if one carefully analyses the booklets and diaries she left behind, one can see, next to meaningless phrases, unlimited series of numbers, listed one above the other, with letters beside them. It is clear that Jicky was aware of cryptography. Until the 1960s, from the dawn of history until the introduction of the internet, this science has always been fundamental in espionage, especially military espionage, and from the uncommon way Jicky took notes, one can assume that she had a thorough knowledge of the subject.

David Kahn, one of the world's leading cryptography experts, states that:

> Code descriptions constitute the most important source of secret information in the world today. It provides information that is far greater in quantity and reliability than spies can provide, and which has a great influence on government policy.

Cryptographic analysis was estimated to have saved a year of war in the Pacific, yet the chronicles only mention it in passing. In Churchill's great history of the Second World War, any reference to the information the Allies obtained through communications analysis has been removed (except for the reference to such information made in the narrative of the American enquiry into Pearl Harbor), even though Britain considered this news source vital enough to assign 30,000 people to it.

The history of the intelligence services in the Second World War has never been written.[18]

With this in mind, from the fact that Jicky worked permanently in the British embassy in Brussels and Paris dealing with intelligence, not to mention the way she jotted down information in her personal diaries, one can easily deduce that she was aware of cryptography, codes and how to conceal the words in plain text. The original message would be written as normal, before being secretly transformed, preferably corresponding to the mother tongue of the message's composer.

In 1920, the Anglo-Americans invented the term cryptanalysis, which later became cryptographic analysis. Cryptology is the science that encompasses both cryptography and decryption (principles of decryption), but the term 'cryptology' generically designates a dual function, both that of securing messages and that of deriving information from them.[19] In *Henry V*, Shakespeare mentions the word 'interception', when the Duke of Bedford, Henry's brother, talks to two gentlemen about a plot against the king by three other nobles. 'The king hath note of all that they intend// By interception which they dream not of,' says Bedford.[20] In this case, he is talking about intercepted letters, as Shakespeare was well aware that, in those days, letters were always being opened and checked. One conspiracy uncovered by cryptanalysis of messages was that of Mary, Queen of Scots, and the most famous story written about cryptanalysis is *The Gold-Bug* by Edgar Allan Poe.

In more recent times, an actress famous in Hollywood for her beauty and bravura, Eva Maria Kiesler, aka Hedy Lamarr, was discovered to be an expert in cryptography. During the Second World War, this Austrian-born Jewish actress created a system to encrypt radio communications, having come up with the invention while researching a system to prevent enemy radio signals from deflecting torpedoes in naval clashes, causing them to miss their target.

Even from this example, it is clear how cryptography played a key role in world history until 1970, before the proliferation of modern espionage technologies. After all, writes Kahn:

Cipher language is the language of spies, condemned to whispering. Success, the very life of an agent, depends on being able to go unnoticed. But the spy must transmit news, otherwise he is of no use. So he resorts to codes, emptied heels, sympathetic inks, microscopic reduction of messages: all steganographic systems to disguise the very fact that a message is being sent. The spy tries to communicate without being noticed.[21]

***

Jicky never showed off, despite the beautiful jewellery and high-fashion clothes. She managed to hide her exuberant personality behind a banal everyday life. Her life was simple, she never flaunted her knowledge. Or her origins.

The small town of Sirolo was divided into two factions. There were those who did not know her personally and who, like bigots, criticised her for being in a relationship with a man much younger than she was. Others, on the other hand, visited her and were fascinated by her. Of the former, she was completely indifferent. *'Aquila non capit muscas,'* as the Latin saying goes: an eagle does not catch flies. Jicky was so far above them that she did not really care. With those she was friendly with, she gave herself completely. Like any great seducer, she could listen for a long time without speaking. She tried to understand her interlocutor's problems by trying to make them feel good, to create an atmosphere of serenity and to show them the solution.

This created a kind of Pavlov effect. Whoever knew her was better off and kept an eye out for her, be it woman, man, young or old. Everyone wanted to be her friend. She dominated everyone who came into contact with her, even if she did everything that she could to show herself to be a normal lady.

Jicky was inconspicuous, even though she had, in fact, created a kind of salon in Sirolo, a cultural circle made up of many foreigners living in the area, including people from Bologna and Milan who had bought a house on the Conero Riviera for their summer holidays. None of them knew exactly what work Jicky did. They saw her as an eccentric English intellectual with whom they could exchange cultural conversations. What is more, no one knew exactly what she did in London so often, apart from shopping for her antique business, nor of the existence of her diaries and an address book. It was all secret.

Chapter 8

Jicky's Diaries and Personal Address Book

Jicky kept her booklets well guarded in an antique box of burnished metal, engraved with squiggles and hidden in her bedroom. According to the diaries and the small address book containing the neatly collected names and addresses of her contacts, when she went to London, Jicky stayed at the four-star Portobello Hotel at 22 Stanley Gardens, Notting Hill. According to the hotel's official website, in 2016 it received the *Good Hotel Guide* award for the most romantic hotel. Built in 1971, it has been a favourite place for celebrities from the worlds of music, fashion and entertainment ever since. The *Telegraph's* gossip columnists wrote that several nights of passion between Johnny Depp and model Kate Moss took place there several years ago, reporting that the couple, having taken refuge there, would immerse themselves in the elegant Victorian bathtub filled to the brim with champagne.

Jicky certainly stayed in the hotel because of its proximity to Portobello Road, where the famous antiques market is held. She also visited the Pierrepont Arcade Antique Market, the covered market on the corner of Camden Passage, which specialised in antique books, as well as other shops in Lordship Lane. Other hotels included in her address book are the Britannia Hotel (now the Biltmore Mayfair), at 44 Grosvenor Square, and the Ladbroke Gardens Hotel, at 28-31 Ladbroke Gardens.

At the beginning of her address book, on the hard cover page, are strange numbers, almost codes:

Bank 039.225
C.S. 346.348
S.S.2.13.1199.132.446

Jicky's Diaries and Personal Address Book

Then downwards:

> Paris 205. 04-45
> Sirolo 958,690

They are not telephone numbers, even though they might appear to be. They are not even bank account numbers as she would not have highlighted them if they were.[22]

'C.S.', one might assume, could be the initials for safe deposit box, (*Cassetta di Sicurezza*), but the number next to it would automatically rule it out. Not only that, Jicky was not so clueless as to write the number of a probable safe deposit box prominently on the cover. What could the numbers next to Paris and Sirolo have meant to her? They could be codes to decrypt a system invented by her to hide some information. Or perhaps they are simple lists of accounts. Surely, such a rational and precise person could never have jotted down such data in vain.

If one skips through all the contacts, at the end of the address book are blank pages for notes, where other numbers or codes that are difficult to understand are written down.

> The years are 1973/74
> Oct 59 10,000
> Nov 59 22,000
> Dec 59 14,000
> Jan 59 13,000
> Feb 59 15,000
> ----------------
> 74.000

A similar pattern with different figures appears for 1974/75.

Could these be monthly expenses? The 10,000 could be the old 10,000 lire, but what does the 59 after the word October refer to?

Perhaps to the year '59? That would not make sense as these are diaries from 1973-74.

The enigma deepens if you try to read the following pages. There are words, months, numbers and sums. All seemingly meaningless. One has to wonder whether Jicky wrote down her notes in this way because of the mindset she acquired working for the secret service. Whether it was a way used by the intelligence service at the time or an original method of not being understood by someone, devised by her to throw off the scent. If so, by whom did she not want to be discovered, and why? Perhaps someone more versed in coding would be able to glean a little more information. Or perhaps not.

It perhaps would not have been difficult for Alan Turing, the English mathematician and scientist who managed to decipher German codes during the Second World War, thanks to his mathematical skills. A job made all the more difficult thanks to the German Enigma programme, which generated codes that changed constantly. Turing devised a tool, the Colossus, which was capable of decrypting German codes created with Enigma, and it is estimated that the Second World War was shortened by two years, and that 14 million people were spared from the Nazi massacre thanks to his efforts. Indeed, Turing is considered the pioneer who paved the way towards the digital computer. Unfortunately, Jicky's 'Enigma' has yet to be discovered.

The fact remains that contacts of people and hotels from many places were noted in her address book. From London and Paris, but also from Rome, Bologna, Pesaro and Dublin.

On the A page, one can read the word 'antiques', with a series of names of antique dealers underneath, mostly from London. Then a series of female names, of ladies – she writes – staying in Paris with their addresses.[23] Mme Allard, Mme Auray, or perhaps Anray, the handwriting is difficult to decipher. There is an Aida Abergel, who was a client of Juvénal hotels and a very good friend of Jicky's and Claude's. She took part in Claude's first wedding with Paola.

Under the letter B, the name Jocelyn Ball Baxter, who lived in Washington D.C. appears as the first contact. Then there are the initials BNP, who resided on the Champs Elysées. Next, Suzanne Bureau, and the address. A Cristiane Bocan in Rome on the Aurelia Antica. Dolly and Nives Brivoresi, always in Rome. A Dr Binder, her family doctor, and Dr Boncher in Paris. Heidi Braungardt from Frankfurt. A Baratta in Bologna who had an antique shop there. All with their addresses next to them.

In Rome, she had an acquaintance in Via Anneo Lucano 64, Collu, one can just make out from her microscopic handwriting. Mario and Laura Collu were Claude's first wife Paola's parents.

In Antibes, she then met Madame Chamat and under her address appears a series of two-digit numbers separated by a hyphen. (15-93-... etc.), perhaps the telephone number. There is also the address of her Parisian coiffeur. Jicky always took great care of her appearance.

Under C is the name George Cabon, and next to it the inscription 'Cabinet T.G Sol. 89.45' and the code with a digit and an arrow pointing to the next page. George Cabon was a French friend of Claude's; they met at university at the Law faculty. He worked at a bank. There is a London address, 15 B. Brechin Place.

Obviously, the address of her former lover, Charles Lieber, is also included, and he lived on Madison Avenue in New York.

Under D was Lucienne Durand and her French address: 5 Villa Dancourt, 18th arrondissement, Paris. 'Tante Lucienne' (Aunt Lucienne) was Claude's nanny. Then a Dalla from Bologna, which is definitely not the famous late songwriter, otherwise Jicky would have mentioned it.

The list goes on…

What a varied mosaic of friends and acquaintances surrounded her. Who knows to what world they belonged. What lives they led. What is strange is the fact that Jicky never mentioned the existence of the people in her phone book to her friends. Not even with those closest to her, to whom she told the events of her past life.

Except for her kinship with the Hermès family, which was now public knowledge, and her former lover Charles, Jicky never explained who many people listed in her address book were. Nor did she ever mention the series of annotated numbers.

Yet in her old age, being blessed to the end with a granite memory, she delighted her friends with anecdotes and detailed stories about the protagonists of her past. Her sharp narratives were enormously interesting because they were true, and she enriched her stories with jokes, colours, noises and descriptions of scents.

On reflection, when she recounted an incident, she would give a name to the protagonist, but omit their surname and address, thus removing the possibility of being able to trace them. Absolute privacy was guaranteed. Like a necklace of pearls, all separate but, at the same time, joined together. She was the thread that connected them all.

***

The same happened in the diaries she updated daily. From her notes one can understand the kind of hectic life she led. In December 1971 she stayed on the quiet Conero Riviera, but her travels were very frequent. As early as 3 January the following year, she had painstakingly organised a calendar of trips to half of Europe. She was very active, but also very precise, with a military-like organisation. In fact, it is clear from her diaries that Jicky, only in appearance, led a bohemian existence, surrounded by artists and intellectuals. In reality, everything was as disciplined as life in the army.

On 20 January she wrote that it was her beloved Paolo's birthday. Nothing in the world would have kept her away from the Marche that day, and they went to lunch in Ancona to celebrate. Then she added: 'cinema' with a question mark beside it. But the appointment is cancelled by a sharp pencil stroke. They would have had better things to do. In the evening, they would be in San Severino Marche.

Throughout these years, Jicky travelled constantly across Europe, to Bologna, Milan, Paris, London and back again. Whether for work or leisure, she seemed to be always on the move.

From the excitement of her movements, the following can be drawn: Jicky was not the simple, retired old English lady who, as a hobby and to fill her days in Sirolo, had opened an antiques business in Numana. True, she had relatives in Paris. It is also understandable that she had to travel to London to purchase items for her antique shop. But not so frequently. It is unclear what all these movements, one after the other, were for. The whole thing was rather bizarre. A dealer who buys pieces in another country normally goes abroad two or three times a year. Certainly not every twenty days or so.

It is not at all clear from the diaries what the rest of her activities were. What was she doing so frequently in London? Even if only for a few days. Why was she commuting between Paris and London before returning to Italy? Was she visiting her son and relatives? Why did she often pass through Milan before going to Bologna and back to Ancona? All this remains unexplained. She transcribed on the front of the sheet the place where she went. But what trips she actually made are difficult to discover, despite the traces of names left here and there on the pages, close to the locations.

On 3 July, at 3 pm, she wrote the word India for the first time. With a number beside it. And a name. Ivan. Then some things she had to do, including call her son. In the following pages, more expenses. Then on 4 July, India again, with a figure next to it. Was it a quote for a trip she had in mind? The next day, more personal expenses: brown lined gloves, nightgowns. The word India again.

On 12 September 1975, she departed for Rimini, from where she travelled to London. It was from London that she organised and planned her trip to India. She contacted Air India, the national airline, for information, and bought books such as *India Novels*. She met with a John B. Or did she? There was a question mark next to it. She also wrote the name 'Liz' with Nepal next to it. Was this someone who was to give her information about Nepal, which she might want to visit, as well as India.

On 13 September she was in Portobello, on Saturday, the day of the historic market. She transcribed a number of items she bought and then went to the bank. Then she wrote the word Nepal. Several times the words 'black moss' appear. Was this the natural perfumery product with a perturbing smell, the black moss of Kashmir, produced from the underbelly of deer, or the geographical area near West Yorkshire? Most likely it was the warm and intoxicating scent she wanted to buy, given Jicky's passion for distinctive fragrances.

The question that arises is: what would she be doing in India? Holiday? Hardly. She would have gone with Paolo, even though he did not like to travel, having gone with her once to Yugoslavia, which he did not enjoy. Shopping for items for the antique shop? A woman alone would not venture on such a far away trip, although of course, she did not know the word fear. Visiting her son? Maybe. Claude travelled for work and was a correspondent for the French news agency, France-Presse, meaning he was forced to live abroad for a lot of the time. He certainly spent many years in South Africa, in Cape Town. It is also known that he spent much time in Rabat and that the Moroccan regime had expelled him because of the French foreign policy stance. It is not known whether he had ever been a correspondent from India, but he did work in Pakistan. Surely Jicky had visited him in Islamabad where he was a correspondent for AFP.

Or had Jicky been sent to India to perform some special and extremely sensitive task? A suspicious Indian resident in Italy, when asked for comment on Jicky's journey to India, mischievously suggested that the British government might have tasked her to check how the territories and cities in the former British colony had developed over the years since independence. Or to observe and report some other kind of information. Her journey involved too many quick stops in such a short time. Like visiting Europe and spending one day in Paris, another in

London and the next in Rome. Without logic and without sense. You do not have time to see anything. Such a conspiracy hypothesis, however, seems rather bizarre. Although, coincidentally, Stella Rimington also joined MI5 after she had moved to India from England.

It would seem, from the notes, that Jicky undertook this trip to India simply because she was curious to visit many places she had long heard about, perhaps at the embassy, as a former colony and part of British history. And to join her son.

Sure enough, she kept compiling lists with the expenses made. With the addition of train fares to Rome and travel costs to London. She would stay twenty days in India, she wrote, jotting down the dates with sums beside them. In the following pages, her hectic life before leaving for India can be seen. Once again there were rounds in Camerano and Ancona. In Porto Civitanova. Everything resumed in the usual manner. It is tender to see that on 23 October she wrote that she had to buy more lipstick. These flirtatious and extremely feminine aspects softened her strong personality, which, in reality, hid a tender soul.

Who knows why a secret agent is always seen as being cynical, calculating and two-faced, capable of holding back their emotions? Perhaps we are influenced by the various spy films. Jicky was noble in her feelings, even if an armour as thick as the bark of an oak tree hid them for protection.

On 30 October, she took a Pan Am flight from Rome Fiumicino, which she reached from Ancona by bus, and arrived in New Delhi at 6 am on 31 October. On the following pages there are charges with an 'r' next to them, possibly rupees, the Indian currency. She transcribed the name of a hotel, probably the Rembagh Palace or Rembayh Palace. Then, after 9 pm, she was in Jaipur, the capital of Rajasthan, nicknamed the Pink City because of the pinkish hues of its buildings. Pink is the symbol of the capital with its fairytale palaces and dreamy hotels.

Jicky continued her journey. On 2 November she travelled to Agra, in northern India (State of Uttar Pradesh). Here she would visit the Taj

Mahal, the famous mausoleum built in 1632 by the Mughal emperor Shah Jahan in memory of his favourite wife. Jicky could not miss a visit to this place, considered among the greatest beauties of Muslim architecture in India and one of the UNESCO World Heritage Sites. Since 2007 it has been listed among the new seven wonders of the world. In the evening, she would still be in Agra – she made a note in her diary.

The next day, Monday, 3 November, she travelled to Bharatpur, the capital of the Bharatpur district and the Bharatpur division of the once princely state of Rajasthan. The city and fort of Bharatpur were built by Maharaja Suraj Mal in the early seventeenth century. In 1805, the state became a British protectorate and remained so until India's independence in 1947.

In the afternoon, at 3 pm, she planned a visit to Akbar's tomb in Sikandra, a suburb of Agra in Uttar Pradesh. It is a masterpiece of Mughal architecture, built between 1605 and 1613. It was Akbar the Great himself who started the construction around 1600, following the Tatar tradition according to which one had to plan the outfitting of one's tomb while alive.

By the evening of 3 November, Jicky was back in Delhi. On Tuesday, 4 November, she flew to Nepal, the largest Himalayan state in Asia. She noted: '1096 in Nepal'. At 9 pm she wrote that she was in the capital, Kathmandu, which has always been considered the centre of Nepal's history, art, culture and economy. A trip to the capital could not be missed.

On Wednesday, 5 November, she was still in the capital. In the morning, she wrote an almost incomprehensible word in her diary with a number and an abbreviation next to it. She spent the day there, perhaps doing some shopping. The next day, 6 November, she was in Bhadgaon or Bhaktapur, an ancient Newari city in the east of the Kathmandu valley, probably founded in the ninth century. In the afternoon she went to Patan, known as Lalitpur, one of the oldest royal cities in the Kathmandu valley, also a UNESCO World Heritage Site. Then in the evening she was back in Kathmandu. The pace of her journey was increasingly convulsive. Adrenalin-pumping. Such a busy schedule is always striking. Almost fascinating.

The following day, 7 November, her birthday, she went to the Patan Zoo. In the afternoon, she left the Indian state of Benares, which was also dependent on the United Kingdom from 1775 to 1948. Among the professed religions, besides Hinduism and Catholicism, Anglicanism is also recognised. The state of Benares is described as princely and is part of the Indian subcontinent. The city of Banaras, which also answers to the names Varanasi, Benares or Kashi, is the oldest continuously inhabited city in the world. According to the Hindu religion, if you die in Banaras you instantly attain liberation from the cycle of birth and rebirth and achieve reunion with the divine nature.

In Benares, people from all over the world arrive to spend their last days of life and death. In this city on the banks of the Ganges River, stands the Manikarnika Ghat, India's largest cremation centre. Seventy thousand bodies a year are cremated here, with ceremonies taking place at all hours of the day and night.

In fact, Jicky included among her appointments at 7 pm on 7 November, the word cremation, i.e. to go and see the ceremony. The ritual is interesting as it involves a series of touching steps. The body is carried by male relatives in a coffin through the streets to the cremators, who perform the cremation. From the windows, children fly colourful kites in the sky. All this in the open, for all to see, which is also why it is a source of attraction for tourists.

Jicky could not miss the event. Her boundless curiosity made her get over the fact that it was her 62nd birthday and that perhaps she should have celebrated elsewhere, rather than witnessing some grim funeral event, of lifeless bodies burnt on a pyre covered with logs. The other interesting thing about this day is that she made an appointment that afternoon to see some people she knew. How is it possible that a 62-year-old well-to-do English lady knew someone in Benares, India apart from her son? Was he with her? Another great mystery.

On Saturday, 8 November, she went to the sacred river Ganges. In the evening, she was in Benares, as well as the following Sunday morning. In the afternoon she moved on. She had a flight to Calcutta. On Monday, 10 November, after carefully writing down on a page the expenses for room, dinner and breakfast, she flew to the federal state of West Bengal. There, a car would be waiting to take her to Darjeeling. The city was situated on the heights of the Shivalik Mountains, the foothills of the Himalayas. During the British Empire in India, Darjeeling, thanks to its temperate climate, was a popular mountain tourist centre for westerners escaping the summer sultriness of the plains. Undoubtedly, Darjeeling is best known for giving its name to the delicious black tea, called the champagne of teas, Jicky's favourite. In fact, it was the only tea she drank. Woe betides if she was offered English Breakfast tea, for example, which she ironically described as 'a bricklayer's tea'.

On 11 November, she hiked Tiger Hill, also in Darjeeling, which is one of the highest peaks in the region and was later the scene of the violent battle in 1999, the Kargil War between India and Pakistan. In the evening, she travelled back to Darjeeling.

The next day she returned to the airport in Bagdogra and took a flight to Calcutta. At 8 pm, she wrote in pen: 'Calcutta-President'. Was this the name of a hotel or was she meeting a president?

On 13 November, at 9.30 am, she left for Bhubaneswar, the capital of the district of Khordha, in the federated state of Orissa, the largest city and an important economic and religious centre in eastern India. A car was waiting to take her to Puri, in the Bay of Bengal, 60 kilometres south of the capital, Bhubaneswar. The city is a favourite pilgrimage destination for Hindus as it is where the Jagannath Temple is located. It is also a favourite because according to the religion, it is the pilgrimage that a Hindu must make at least once in his life.

On Friday, 14 November, she paid a visit to Konark, a town also located in the Puri district. Konark is home to the Temple of the Sun, a religious building dating back to the thirteenth century and an important shrine for Brahmanism, which was also listed as a UNESCO World Heritage Site in 1984. In the evening, she was back in Puri.

On Sunday, 16 November, Jicky took a plane to Madras, present-day Chennai, the capital city of the federated state of Tamil Nadu and an important commercial centre with a rich cultural and artistic heritage. She visited the city by taxi before heading for the beaches. In the evening, she returned to the city.

On Tuesday, 18 November, she left at dawn and flew from Madras to Madurai in Tamil Nadu, where she visited a temple. A car took her to the centre of Thekkady, then after jeep ride, she hiked to the famous lake in the Periyar National Park, a protected natural area in the mountains of Kerala, in the land of the gods. With a lake at its heart, the area is also a tiger reserve, while tourists also come to admire Indian elephants bathing by the Periyar Lake.

The next day, she hired a car again to take her to Kottayam, 117 kilometres away, where the nearest railway station was located. As always, Jicky did not lose her biting humour, commenting that the driver of the car accompanying her was 'very bad'. The journey must not have been too pleasant for her given the negative assessment. From Kottayam, she then went to Cochin, 85 kilometres away. It was certainly not an easy journey. Exhausting to say the least. Almost tracing the hectic pace of her life. The myriads of places she visited in a short space of time gives an idea of what kind of rhythm she still managed to keep up at the age of 62. What an extraordinary temperament she had.

On Friday, 21 November, she took the plane to Bangalore, the capital and largest city of the state of Karnataka. It is currently famous for the success of its highly technologically developed IT companies. At 8 pm the same day, she moved on to Mysore, the second largest city in Karnataka, which is also considered to be the state's cultural capital.

She spent 23 November in Somnathpur, on the Kaveri River, a small town 35 kilometres from Mysore. There she would have visited the famous Keshava Temple, which is also considered an important site for archaeological heritage and is a magnet that attracts tourists from all over the world. The following day, she hired a car to take her back to Bangalore, where she would catch a flight to Bombay. On Wednesday, 26 November, at around 2 pm, she flew to Udaipur, one of the cities in the federated state of Rajasthan, known as city of lakes. Its fame lies in its marvellous palaces from the Rajput era, many of which have been converted into luxury hotels. The next day, to maintain her usual frenzy, she took a flight to Delhi, where she stayed for a short time.

Friday, 28 November saw her boarding another plane, this time to Ellora. Since ancient times, Ellora has been an important pilgrimage centre for three major religions: Buddhism, Brahmanism and Jainism. It enjoys an important artistic flowering, especially in the field of architecture. Jicky wrote in her diary that at 12 noon she visited the caves of Ellora, a UNESCO-protected site, 29 kilometres from the city of Aurangabad, in the state of Maharashtra. There are in fact thirty-four caves used as temples, created by excavations in the rock.

She flew to Bombay on Saturday, 29 November. She planned to spend all day at the beach, so marked it in her diary, 'Juhu Beach', which is located near a posh resort. Then she planned to do some shopping, probably in the nearby small shops.

Her last flight was scheduled for the night of 29/30 November and took her from Bombay to Rome, arriving in the morning at around 10 am. She took a train at 2.45 pm and arrived at 6.45.

On the bottom page she transcribed all the things she brought from India: clothes, two pairs of sandals, blue shoes, white silk, chemise, tea, films, children's games. She also added a list detailing the costs of the trip. Whatever the amount, it was money well spent, for a trip of a 1,001 nights. She also dedicated a small page to her own 'desires', a wish list.

What she would probably like to buy. Disks, two brown bags, Gucci? (with a question mark beside it). Indian books. Limoges saucers. In Paris? (trip to be decided). Pillows with her son's name next to them, presents for him. Many books. One by the writer Carlo Castellaneta with Rizzoli publishing house next to it. Then the book, *Gli ermellini neri*, (*Black Ermines*), the novel by Michele Prisco, which must have been recommended to her. A clear sign that she was now reading books in Italian without difficulty and that she had mastered the language.

Then, on 1 December, she may have returned to work, as she resumed compiling long lists of items with a number next to them, presumably the price, including items such as a silver box, two glasses, etc.

On the 2nd, she began to organise her Christmas preparations. What dedication she poured into the greeting cards to be sent, especially for all the English people, who send them long in advance. She made a list of who to send them to, then prepared another list with photographs of the beach in Puri, of the girl with the shells, several taken in Delhi, especially ones of the Red Forte Mosque and the Delhi Fort, another UNESCO heritage site. It was probably a list of the photographs she wanted to have printed. Then on the following pages, more lists of names, probably of friends and acquaintances, because there are no surnames beside them. Next, lists and lists full of nouns with numbers, figures next to them, all in lower case with blue and red pen.

She probably spent Christmas at home as there are no other travel plans marked. On the 29th, she would be in Ancona with Paolo and organised New Year's Eve dinner with him. Tortellini, zampone (pig's trotter), cake, lentils – all noted down. She conformed perfectly to the Italian culinary tradition, to please her companion with his distinctly local tastes. There was no trace at this time of Christmas pudding, the typical English Christmas cake that she adored.

On the 31st, the last day of the year, she was once again in Ancona with Paolo and, in the evening, partying. It was New Year's Eve after all. Another year had ended. In the agenda, the usual ambiguities were noted down. Lists, numbers, acronyms and words.

***

In her old age, Jicky often went back to read her diaries. Almost like looking through an album of old photographs. She had all her memories imprinted on those sheets of paper, in her famous diaries. She loved them. And she would read them again and again. Then, out of the blue, when she met one of the people from her past, immortalised forever with biro on the white pages, she would say to them: 'We had lunch together on 6 July twenty years ago.' Her booklets and photographs, as well as her letters, kept her company in the last years of her life in Sirolo. Allowing her to cling to distant days. Everything was perfectly preserved. For each person dear to her, she kept a kind of folder where she kept every memory of them. Holiday postcards, letters, zodiac sign books and photographs. Almost a tribute. She filed everything, even material that one would not expect, banal in appearance.

From the 1977 diary, we learn of a trip she made to Scotland in September. She stayed at the Balmoral Hotel, a very luxurious, historic Victorian hotel, and on the 29th, after a quick trip to the bank, she visited Edinburgh, went to the tourist centre and bought a Scottish cashmere coat. Another passion of Jicky's. In the evening, she stayed in a different hotel, probably on Dundas Street. On 1 October, a visit to the antiques fair and the 'Assembly Room', where many art exhibitions, concerts and festivals were held.

She flew back to Milan on 7 October. Once back in Sirolo, she continued with her tours of the surroundings and her various appointments. At the end of the month, she made a note in her diary: 'plan next trip'. This was how her life always unfolded. She organised, left, returned and left again. She never stayed in one place for long. Never the same old grind.

On 4 November, she took the train to Bologna and wrote in her diary: parrot. Perhaps it is here that she acquired the enormous, noisy bird, Coco, who for many years lived with her in her house, frightening unsuspecting guests who came into the living room, unaware of his comical speech and horror movie screams.

Then it was off again, meetings, trips to the bank, visits to Mimi, (who could this be?), planning flights to London, another back to Paris. On 20 November, she planned a train to Ancona. On the 25th, she was back in Bologna. A series of people to meet noted. On 7 December, she made pen sketches of a sofa. Then back to Milan. London. Lists of expenses. Names to meet.

***

Had she not recorded her past so precisely in her diaries, no one would ever believe the gruelling progress of the days of this elegant, quiet-looking Englishwoman. Jicky had always enjoyed very good health and suffered from very few ailments, with only a few hip problems that required surgery when she was an old woman. She never had any serious illnesses, although she had contracted malaria in the past during one of her travels. She had come out of it very well, however, apart from a bit of a cyclical fever. As if a simple mosquito could have stopped her!

She proudly declared that an Englishman was stronger than anyone else. 'An Englishman never complains because there is a draught or because some draught may cause some disturbance,' she said. For her, being English meant being strong. And long-lived. She had an aunt who had lived to be 105, without any major ailments. Until the end of her life, when she was nearly 98, she always maintained the lively vitality of a young girl. She never saw a doctor, and only in the last years of her life, when she was very ill, did one visit her – and she still made flirtatious remarks about the handsome doctor to her friends.

Throughout her life, she always refused to take dual nationality, English-French or English-Italian. This was a great disadvantage for her, especially in old age. In fact, she was precluded from accessing the Italian national health service. For every hospital stay, medicine taken or doctor visited, she had to pay out of her own pocket. She did not even have the right to vote. As far as Jicky was concerned, she was born English, and she would die English. She was a proud Englishwoman, a descendant of a people who had dominated the world with their colonies and empire. She did not worry about diseases; they did not frighten her. 'We have to die of something anyway,' she repeated, smiling.

It was the same for the English language, the British version was the only one that mattered. Other nations like the United States or Australia or New Zealand spoke English, but not as well as the British. George Bernard Shaw, the Irish writer, playwright and linguist, said that the Americans had not spoken English in America for decades. A clear allusion that their language, American, could not be as sophisticated as that of the British. He also famously said that the British and the Americans were two countries separated by a common language.

Churchill had gone further by saying that learning English at school had been a noble thing: 'By being so long in the lowest form (at Harrow School) I gained an immense advantage over the cleverer boys. They all went on to learn Latin and Greek and splendid things like that. But I was taught English... Thus, I got into my bones the essential structure of the ordinary British sentence, which is a noble thing.' Jicky was on the same wavelength, although she loved both Greek and Latin, just as Churchill did. Among the English-speaking languages, however, only British English was right for her. There was simply no other.

Jicky was not just from Britain. She was Britain.

Chapter 9

Nicoletta, Nicole or Nico

'You see, Nicoletta, British English is the best.' Jicky ran her fingers through the air, her hands in an inverted V and forearms up, drawing the roof of a house. 'It is like a house with several floors. On the ground floor, there are Australians and New Zealanders. On the first floor, the Americans. And above them all, on the top floor, the British.'

In a few words, Jicky had explained the essence of the English language spoken in England and British culture to the young student in her shop. By using the description of a mansion, she had managed to explain her thoughts.

The girl listened attentively to this distinguished lady, whom she had met by chance and who pronounced English with a typically upper-class accent. She spoke in a refined manner and, although seated on a small armchair in the shop, her shoulders were upright and she maintained an authoritative manner.

Nicoletta had entered Jicky's antique shop almost by chance one day. She had browsed through the flood of objects and furniture and, attracted by an antique pink Victorian toilet set, she had then ended up buying two old picture frames in need of restoration.

From that day on, the two women had started speaking English to each other all the time. Nicoletta attended the scientific secondary schools and soon afterwards would move to Florence to undertake four years of study at the Superior School for Interpreters and Translators. From there, she would enrol at IULM, the University of Milan (Languages and Communication Department) for another four years.

From the day when she bought the picture frames, Jicky and Nicoletta started to see each other regularly in the shop. In addition to conversing in English, Nicoletta made Jicky read and correct her English homework. The corrections were carefully made, right down to the commas, and took a long time, sometimes the whole afternoon.

Then suddenly, one day Jicky made a strange request: 'write a few lines by hand on some sheets of paper!' Nicoletta obeyed, unaware of the real motives, not imagining what was behind the demand. She thought it was just a bizarre request from an even more bizarre English lady.

The pair soon became friends and a mother-daughter relationship was established, with the difference being that Nicoletta could confess things to this English mother that are usually kept hidden from real mothers, like first loves, crushes, problems with classmates or friends. Jicky was ready to give her advice, to explain how the world worked. She had become a life teacher for her. Besides being a well of cultural knowledge, she had the ability to foresee events thanks to either her life experiences or because of the witty reasoning she had developed over the years. When Jicky advised Nicoletta to stop hanging around with a certain group of friends because they were unsuitable for her, in the end she was always completely right.

Jicky switched from calling her Nicoletta to calling her Nicole, which itself soon became Nico, although when pronounced in English, it sounded like Nicow. Jicky was always kind to Nicoletta, even if, in the case of behaviour she thought was wrong, or 'inappropriate', she did not scruple to rebuke her harshly for her own good, she said. Just like a real mother. What she absolutely did not tolerate, however, was the pronunciation of English. Nicoletta knew a fellow student in Florence, Sabra, an Italian-American, so after a while, she had started using American-English idioms and words. This was bad news. Jicky became nervous hearing them and would get angry.

'Bullshit? What is this horrible word?' She scolded her irritably, but always in sophisticated English. 'Jicky, it's a word I often hear at school from an Italian-American friend of mine,' replied the young woman, almost apologetically. 'A young lady should never use those words... you can't lower yourself to that!' she rebuked her.

In addition to studying the language, as well as her love for William Shakespeare and English, French and Russian novelists, Jicky gradually educated her on other matters. How to recognise in a minute, for example, whether a person is lying or telling the truth. Nicoletta was amused by these lessons. She never imagined, however, that she was dealing with a former British Secret Service agent, who was among the best equipped to analyse the personality of the individual in front of her.

'Sometimes, facial expressions don't accurately express a person's true feelings. One may be faced with an individual with sad eyes, but that does not mean that he really is sad,' Jicky explained one day. 'One must not let oneself be influenced by the apparent appearance but analyse deeper. Facial expressions and posture are important. Sometimes there are people who have more self-control of how they express themselves.'

She continued with her explanations:

It is not true that a person with a depressed expression really is. We don't all have intuitable facial expressions. There are individuals that are easier to decipher and others, less so. Less obvious. Each of us has a different way of expressing their emotions. Someone may have a few tics, a sudden movement, like rubbing an eye when lying or shifting their gaze to the side, but we are by no means all the same. Therefore, one has to consider the context one is in, whether one is looking directly at one's face or avoiding eye contact, one's body posture and, above all, one's voice.

Nicoletta listened, a little perplexed, to the instructions she received. 'Is that true?' she thought. Then, years later, when Nicoletta was working in a parliamentary group press office in Rome, the two women were watching the news together in the large dining room of her house when Jicky said out of the blue: 'Do you see that important party leader from the North, Umberto Bossi, who is doing an interview in front of the cameras?'

'Yes, Jicky, so?'

'Behind him is one of his party comrades. Look! Although he's smiling, he's leaning forward, look how he looks at him sideways through his red glasses. He hates him! He's envious of him. He's staring at him sideways, he's not looking straight at the camera, look, look...'

'No, Jicky,' replied Nicoletta, 'he's a loyal party companion, a right-hand man, a colonel. You're wrong.'

'That man will betray him!' she thundered, confidently.

Never was a prediction more apt. After a few years, the man did betray him.

Chapter 10

My Friend Dorothy

In those days, Jicky had a trusted English friend in Sirolo, Dorothy Craggs Varty. Only in the last years of her life, however, did a series of phantom 'girlfriends' appear around her, many of whom were mere acquaintances who would visit her at home, or run a few errands for her, when, aged over 90, Jicky no longer went out. Some were from Sirolo and others from abroad. Only Dorothy, however, was considered to be her only true, best friend; the one she liked to hang out with and confide in the most. They had been friends for years, and so Jicky had immediately introduced Dorothy to Nicoletta.

Dorothy was a beautiful, petite lady born in 1930 in Danby Wiske, North Yorkshire, with very fair skin, blonde hair and an infectious cheerfulness. She married Tom Varty and moved to Darlington, where her husband played football for Darlington FC. In 1952, after Tom stopped playing, they owned a small supermarket until they moved to Hurworth. Tom became a milkman and Dorothy a travel agent, which gave her a love of travelling. In 1984 they moved to London. When she became a widow in 2010, Dorothy moved to live by the sea in Whitstable.

Tom was a typical English gentleman who dressed in tweed and was always accompanied by his bull terrier, Ben. Dorothy and Tom were the parents of a famous fashion designer, Keith Varty,[24] who was employed by Byblos. Dorothy used to attend all Keith's shows and never missed any, whether they were in Paris when he was a designer for Dorothee Bis, in Milan, or in other cities. After the shows she would meet all the supermodels, including Jerry Hall.

Keith and his partner Alan, also a designer, had bought the most beautiful villa on Monte Conero, which they had furnished themselves, and Dorothy, Tom and their two other daughters, Susan and Andy, would spend long periods in Sirolo during the summer months. Tom Ford often visited Sirolo to see Keith and Alan, when he first started working for Gucci, always staying in their villa.

Jicky had a lot of fun in that environment. In their beautiful mansion at the top of Monte Conero, which seemed almost suspended in the void, interesting people would arrive from London, including famous antique dealers and eccentric friends. Keith and Alan lived in complete luxury. Jicky amusedly used to say, 'Do you know that it took 2 billion lire just to design the garden surrounding their villa, and the most famous garden architect in Italy was called from Bologna?' The grounds were fantastic. There was a swimming pool in the garden, embedded in the ground, almost like a natural pond with a regular shape.

'Once,' Jicky recounted, with the enthusiasm of a young girl, 'Keith organised a surprise birthday party for his mother, Dorothy. It was a marvel. A charter flight from London landed at Falconara airport carrying all the guests. It was an incredible party. Music, servants in oriental costumes, a series of surprises and delicious food specially flown in. A party of a thousand and one nights!'

Jicky would often visit Dorothy and Tom. Or Dorothy would drop by her house and they would wash each other's hair like two sisters. Dorothy and Tom did not live in Keith and Alan's villa, but at first stayed in a flat in Numana. Only later did they move into a house a few metres away from the stylists, also on Monte Conero.

When she was already over 90 years old, Jicky re-read in one of her famous diaries a distant date. 'Nico, on 6 July twenty years ago, we went to lunch at Dorothy's house, remember? She was on Avellaneda Street then. You gave me a lift in the car. It was your birthday!'

Until the end, Dorothy remained a dear friend and confidante of Jicky's, until the latter's death in 2011. Dorothy, meanwhile, passed away on 3 June 2024.

In the last years of her life, Dorothy recounted that she was very proud of her dear friend Jicky. She knew who she really was. Jicky used to tell her about her life as a secret agent before going to Sirolo. Dorothy had always been very proud to be her friend.

***

In the meantime, Paolo's presence in Jicky's life was constant and unobtrusive. He was always there, but he was silent. He did not meddle too much in her personal affairs, never saying a word about her movements in London or around the world. He let her do whatever she wanted and would simply go to the shop to pick her up, chat with customers and then disappear. Always in a very discreet manner. He was present, but not too conspicuous. Jicky was really in love with him, although it was hard to understand how a somewhat chubby man, who was not very tall and did not have a great education, had made her lose her head so much. Certainly, according to her stories, Paolo was very emotional and passionate.

Jicky always said that Paolo was seventeen years younger than her, but that was not the case. The sums did not add up, and Paolo only discovered this after reading her identity papers when Jicky was hospitalised. If Jicky was born in 1913 and Paolo in 1939, the age difference between the two was twenty-six years, not seventeen, a fact that Jicky had managed to keep hidden for decades. Paolo was almost shocked when he heard about it.

Jicky showed courage in being able to live with such a huge, but at the same time harmless, lie. It would not have been difficult for a secret agent to keep such a secret for so many years. After all, she had been trained to live in mysteries, to be able to conceal her true personality and to have many parallel lives. A double face. Or rather, a thousand faces.

To survive, once in the hands of the Nazis, the only weapon available to the agents was the art of lying. It was part of their required skill set. The better they were at deceiving the Nazis, the greater the chances of survival for the agent and the Resistance groups to which they belonged. Indeed, one of Winston Churchill's favourite maxims was that 'In wartime, is truth not so precious that she should always be attended by a bodyguard of lies?'

It was so in wartime. The same would be true in love.

No one ever suspected anything. Jicky was very clever at lying in such a small town like Sirolo for so many years. On the other hand, however, in interpersonal relationships, she was a sincere and straightforward person, a true friend. Her love for Paolo was so great that she was afraid of losing him. In love and war, every game is allowed, and she would have devised any subterfuge to hide her real age from him. She feared that he would be frightened by the relationship not conforming to society's rules and that he would be intimidated by the harsh criticism of his countrymen. They would cry scandal, and, out of weakness, he might leave her for good. Was it an act of insecurity that contrasted with her strength of character and resolve, or simple realism? She knew him well; he would have left her even though he was very much in love with her. But a curtain of lies would have protected the truth. Just as Churchill advised.

Chapter 11

Nazis

'Nico, one day we were at home and we heard a knock at the door. We went to open it. It was the Nazis...'

For the first time, Jicky began to tell Nicoletta the story of when she was captured by the Nazis. One of the worst days of her life, for her and her partner. However, she omitted the real reasons for the arrest. She did not confide that she was captured because she was an agent of the British Secret Service, but for the first time, she did tell her about the Nazis.

What is a Nazi? To the collective imagination that did not live through those years, from studies done at school, readings afterwards and numerous historical films, a Nazi was a beast. Be it one of the Occupation, the Holocaust, of Dachau or Auschwitz. Of Anne Frank. Of the slaughter of the disabled and mentally ill. Of the mass slaughters. Of Dr Mengele's medical experiments. Of the crime of humanity with 12 million people killed, 6 million Jews. Of the Shoah.

A Nazi was an assassin sanctioned by a uniform. Fierce, ruthless and bloodthirsty, drugged with Pervitin, the 'super soldier' serum, or methamphetamine. In order to be so ruthless and for the inhuman pace they sustained, they apparently used it on a massive scale. If you consider that on 10 May 1940, Hitler and his men launched the Blitzkrieg, and in less than forty-five days occupied Paris, then on 25 June, only a month later, had conquered the whole of France, one can imagine why they used it in inordinate doses. They had conquered four countries and confronted the French army, which was numerically very strong. They devised diabolical concentration camps, involving the extermination of the Jews and the torture of women and children.

Hitler had declared: 'The conspirators? I will hang them like pigs.' He exterminated those who had plotted against him by detonating a bomb in Rastenburg. The convicted conspirators were hung from butchers' hooks as the Führer had ordered. Their long agony was filmed by a cameraman and projected into Hitler's sadistic circle. The Nazis were the protagonists of the darkest period in European history.

Jicky never used any of those adjectives to describe Nazis. Not one derogatory term. Never a comment, an insult, an angry definition, a description to demolish these 'super soldiers'. In her detailed account of the Nazis, her voice was enough to describe their horror, pronouncing the word 'Nazi' almost jerkily, convulsively, desperately. And it was even more clear by the grimace of pain that suddenly appeared on her face, her mouth almost twisted, her face stretched as she uttered the word: naa-zii-sss. The way she said it contained within it all the insults, epithets, disgust and anger she could harbour towards them.

Jicky had been captured and allegedly tortured by the Nazis. Although it is not known for sure, it is highly likely that she was tortured because, after all, this is what happened with all British spies discovered by the Gestapo. It was the practice they used with everyone. She was taken to prison while pregnant, and thrown onto the floor to sleep in the cold, almost to the point of freezing. Exactly what kind of cruelty she was subjected to is not known, but it is imaginable.

Jicky never explicitly recounted the torture, although it is obvious that she had been subjected to it. As discussed earlier, when the nurse who stuck the IV needle into the vein in her arm before she died, Jicky, semi-conscious and in severe pain, called her a Nazi. She always recounted the horror of her capture, but she never described what happened in her cell during the days of her captivity. Nor did she describe how she managed to escape. Nothing but silence.

Why did she take refuge in painful muteness and not speak of the violence she had suffered? Was it out of modesty? Was she ashamed of it? She had lost her dignity in that cell. She would never have been able to say what had happened and reopen the wound. She would never

Young Jicky with her dog.

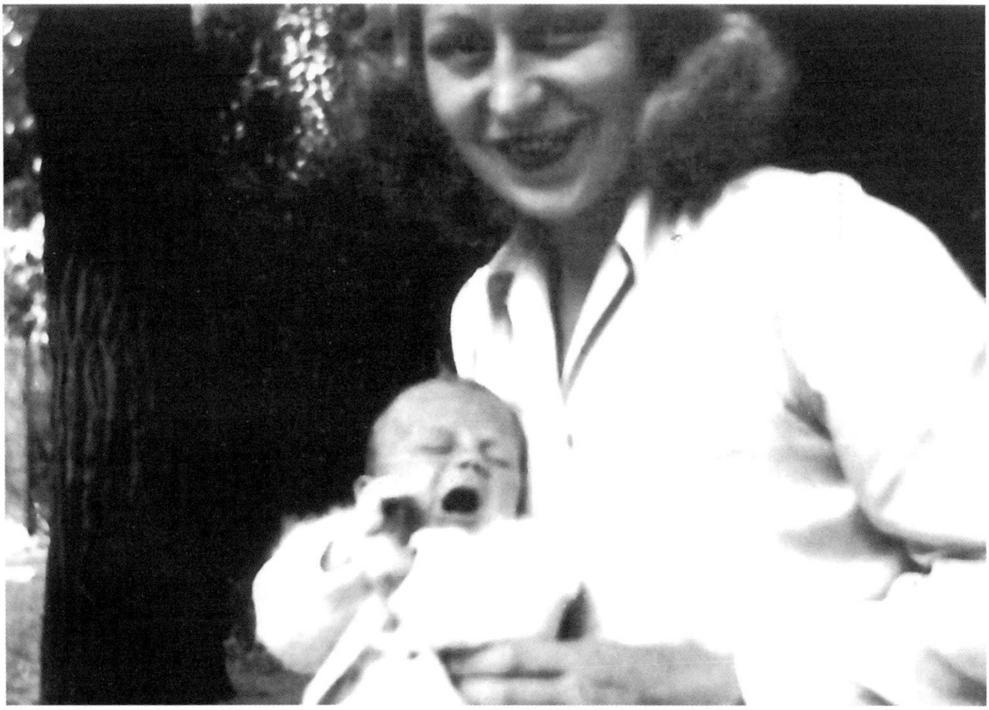

Jicky with her newborn son, Claude.

Left: Jicky teaching Claude to walk.

Below: Jicky in a relaxing moment.

Madame Jicky in Paris with a friend.

Above left: Jicky in Paris.

Above right: Jicky by the sea.

Jicky's diaries and address book.

Jicky's Hermès love letter carrier.

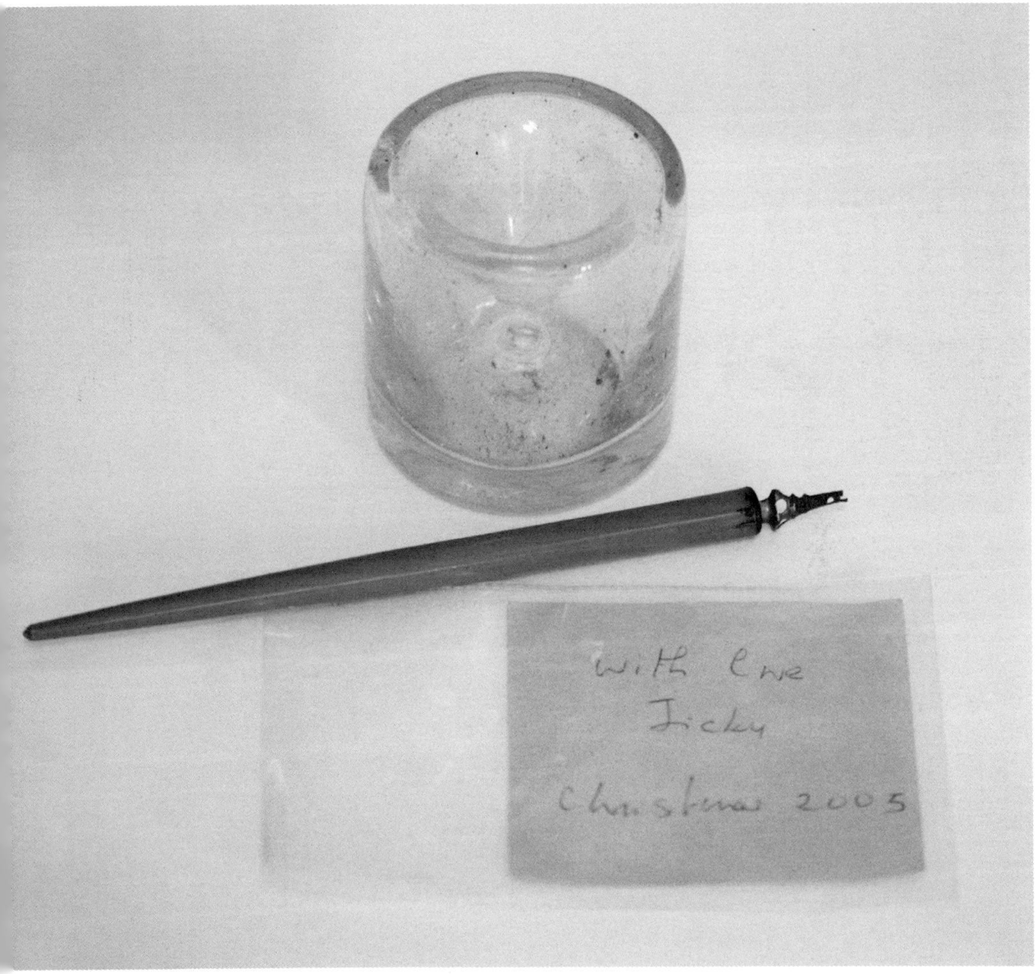

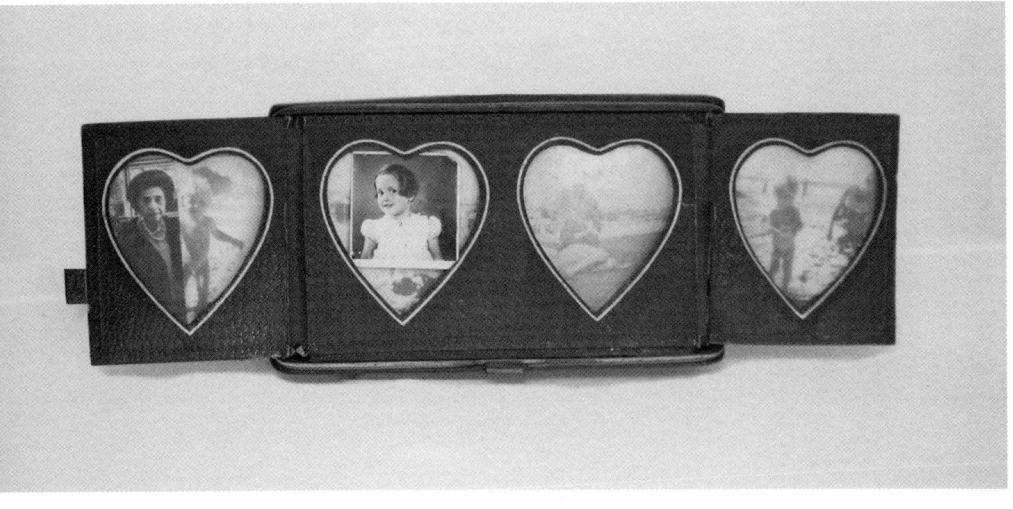

Victorian pen and inkwell from Jicky's collection given to Nicoletta as a Christmas present.

Jicky's travel Dior photo frame with photographs of Pascale as a little girl (centre) and her mother Myriam (left).

Above left: Jicky's Hermès Kelly bag.

Above right: Jicky at home with her dog.

Jicky's house in Sirolo.

Right: Paolo Paolini.

Below: Jicky in her antique shop.

Jicky at Dorothy Varty's suprise sixtieth birthday party, organised by Dorothy's fashion designer son, Keith Varty. Dorothy is seen seated, behind her daughter Andy. Next to Jicky (standing, centre) is Tom Varty, Dorothy's husband, with their dog Ben in front.

Jicky in Sirolo.

Jicky after swimming at the Sirolo beach.

Above left: Jicky on one of her trips, probably in Scotland.

Above right: Jicky joking with her son, Claude.

Jicky at the entrance to her house in Sirolo.

Jicky and Paolo in Sirolo in front of the Conero Mountain.

Jicky during a trip to Scotland with a friend.

British engineer Anthony Piercey.

CERTIFIED COPY OF AN ENTRY OF BIRTH GIVEN AT THE GENERAL REGISTER OFFICE

Application Number 10876366-1

REGISTRATION DISTRICT	ST. ALBANS	
1913 BIRTH in the Sub-district of Harpenden	in the County of Hertford	

Columns:-	1	2	3	4	5	6	7	8	9	10
No.	When and where born	Name, if any	Sex	Name and surname of father	Name, surname and maiden surname of mother	Occupation of father	Signature, description and residence of informant	When registered	Signature of registrar	Name entered after registration
139	Seventh November 1913 Kinkwick Lodge Avenue Harpenden U.D.	Hazel Ursula	Girl	Sydney Herbert Smith	Margaret Emily Smith formerly Ashendon	Shipping Merchant	Margaret Sydney Smith Mother Kinkwick Lodge Harpenden	Third December 1913	N.P. Busby Registrar.	

CERTIFIED to be a true copy of an entry in the certified copy of a Register of Births in the District above mentioned.
Given at the GENERAL REGISTER OFFICE, under the Seal of the said Office, the 30th day of June 2020

BXCJ 018526

CAUTION: THERE ARE OFFENCES RELATING TO FALSIFYING OR ALTERING A CERTIFICATE AND USING OR POSSESSING A FALSE CERTIFICATE ©CROWN COPYRIGHT
WARNING: A CERTIFICATE IS NOT EVIDENCE OF IDENTITY.

Jicky's birth certificate.

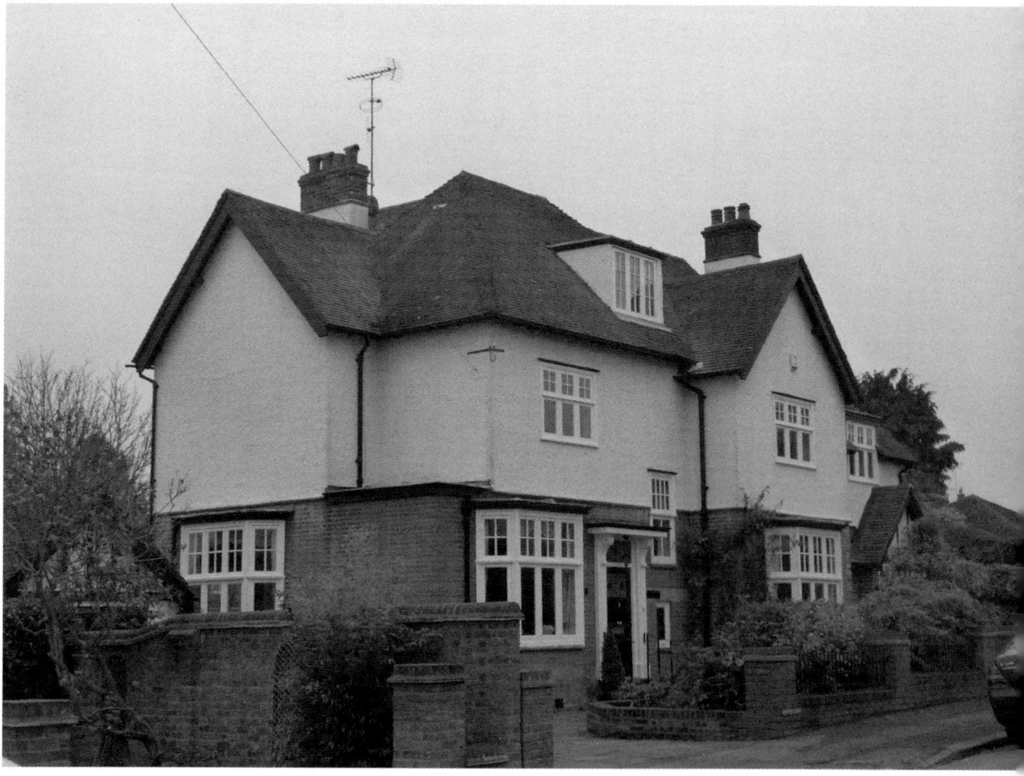

Jicky's house in Harpenden.

Above left: Friends or relatives of Jicky at a garden party.

Above right: Jicky's rag doll, given to her as a child by one of the First World War soldiers billeted in the gardens of her home in Harpenden.

Right: Jicky's grave in Sirolo.

Above: Jicky on another one of her trips, probably in Morocco.

Left: Jicky with her grandson.

Jicky's plaque at her house in Sirolo.

The ceremony for the unveiling of the plaque in Sirolo. From left: Marta Marchetti, Director of Winston Churchill Museum in Montemaggiore al Metauro; Pascale Mussard; Mario Maraschioni, Sirolo Cultural Circle; Cameron Ballester, diplomat from the British Embassy in Rome; Nicoletta Maggi, the author.

The large crowd awaiting the unveiling of the plaque in front of Jicky's home.

Above: Pascale Mussard and Cameron Ballester unveil the plaque.

Left: Dorothy pays homage to Jicky's plaque a couple of months after the unveiling.

have been able to admit that her self-respect as a human being had been torn from her. She was no longer a woman in there. She had been dehumanised. She could not bear to be pitied.

That trauma would accompany her throughout her life. An indelible wound. An unspeakable, immense pain. What were trivial everyday difficulties? Absolutely nothing. If there was no work? 'You invent something new to do or you change country,' she suggested. A serious illness? 'We have to die of something anyway!' If a great love was lost? 'The course of true love never did run smooth,' quoting Shakespeare, or 'It was not true love.'

For a person who had stared death in the face, in the clutches of the Nazis and had managed to survive, everything else in life was simple and solvable. So when she had to qualify a person whom she considered to be the worst of the worst, she naturally called them: Nazi.

Chapter 12

Seize the Moment

'Nico, I'm glad you're organising a painting exhibition in Numana. You've been painting since childhood; it's about time you did something like this. I will be there, count on it.'

Nicoletta was happy about the exhibition. Even more so for Jicky's words of approval. She valued her comments or criticism greatly, often bringing the painted canvases to her home where Jicky, after scrutinising them for a long time, would make her judgements. She appreciated the fact that Nicoletta painted pictures that were 'so different from all the others. Unique.' She liked her watercolours less. 'With so much technique and study, everyone makes beautiful watercolours, but they are all similar, though. Why did you title your exhibition "Seize the Fleeting Moment?"'

Nicoletta showed her the card with the invitation to the exhibition that was to be held a month later at the Municipal Palace in Numana. In front of it, in the foreground, was a photograph of one of her paintings, a landscape immersed in the green countryside, populated by joyful wayfarers and small houses from bygone days. Below the picture, the date of the inauguration with the duration of the exhibition, 11-19 August 1990. On the back of the ticket was an explanation as to why the event was named 'Seize the Fleeting Moment'. It told of an artist intent on painting, who was competing with a ray of sunlight hitting the blank canvas. He wanted to finish the painting before the light darkened the canvas. It was a race against time that finally defeated him, but he had fought to the end, without becoming discouraged. That was seizing the moment for Nicoletta. To never stop fighting until the last second and to be happy in that instant, whatever the outcome.

At the opening of the exhibition, Jicky showed up well dressed and on time. All her life she had visited the exhibitions of the most famous French painters and great artists. She had met Magritte and Bernard Buffet. That evening, even though it was the exhibition of an unknown local artist, who moreover worked in another job and painted as a hobby, as everyone in her family had always done, she showed up with the same attitude. Elegant and proud. As if it was the exhibition of a famous painter.

***

Jicky treated Nicoletta like a daughter, but she did have a son of her own, Claude. A famous journalist in France who lived in Paris, Claude had two children, a boy and a girl, and travelled a lot for work. He had always worked as a correspondent for the major French news agency, AFP, in distant countries. After many years abroad, however, he returned to Paris full time. After divorcing his wife, the mother of his children, he cohabited with a woman much younger than him, who was a princess in her native country in Africa.

Jicky constantly praised her son's professional skills. 'He is a very good journalist,' she proudly declared, 'nothing scares him.' She also said he had a bad temper and was sometimes grumpy and a bit harsh. She liked his new companion, the princess, whom she found interesting and simple. He only visited his mother once a year in Sirolo, often with his children.

However, he did call her every Sunday afternoon to ask how she was and, when Jicky was very old, he worried that she did not have enough money. Jicky did not receive a big pension, only 600 euros a month for contributions paid for her work as an antiquarian. She received nothing from the British government. Perhaps because she had never applied for anything? Claude sent her money to buy wood for the fire, which was the only source of heat in the entire house during the harsh winter months. Their shared strength of character and stubbornness often made them quarrel. Jicky confided later that when he returned to Paris, she could finally breathe a sigh of relief. Her son insisted on cooking in her house, improvising himself as a chef, leaving stains of 'horrible greasy gravy' on the precious period furniture in the living room; something Jicky could simply not tolerate. Her beautiful antiques soiled by tomato splatters. No. That would have been too much for her.

Jicky was very happy when Claude brought her beloved grandchildren to see her. She doted on them. She adored them, she lived thinking about them. Whenever anyone would drop by for a visit, she would keep them talking for hours about the two children and their unique personalities. The boy was quieter, while the girl, on the other hand, was determined and intelligent, with a great personality, even as a child. 'Once,' Jicky remembered, 'she was very stubborn and wanted red ballet shoes. Paolo and I had to go all the way to Porto Recanati to find some and make her happy. She was only 4 years old.'

She was full of praise and compliments for her very special granddaughter, much more than for her brother. Jicky was very proud of her. After compulsory schooling, she enrolled in a faculty to become a film director and producer in Paris. Jicky could not contain her joy. The house was wallpapered with photographs of her grandchildren, especially the little girl, who shared her grandmother's fair complexion. In later years, however, when Jicky was elderly, neither her son nor grandchildren visited her in Sirolo. Not even when she was ill and about to die. The grandchildren did send her letters, however, sometimes with their photographs included.

***

'I'm glad, Nico, that you often go to England and that you have become a member of an influential English club. Nice!' Jicky exclaimed, delightedly. And then: 'Who are Jake Parkinson-Smith and Carlo Carello?' she asked. 'Surely, if you've joined this London club, it means you're planning a future in England?' Jicky reasoned as she held up the black paper envelope with silver lettering from England with Nicoletta's confirmation of acceptance to the club inside. 'But aren't you doing well in Rome with your job as press officer?' she asked her.

'No, Jicky, I don't want to quit my job, just to go to London more frequently. Jake Parkinson-Smith and Carlo Carello are in charge of the exclusive club open only to registered members. Carlo gave me confirmation, they deemed me eligible to attend their club. Officially I am a member now,' Nicoletta replied.

'I love London, too,' Jicky continued. 'What I miss most are the long walks, both in winter and summer, in the parks. I could walk for hours without getting tired in those vast green expanses. In those parks. Wonderful!'

In London, Jicky loved that fairytale atmosphere that comes with Christmas, the liveliness of New Year's Eve, that unmistakable mix between past and present, between tradition and future. She also missed the English milk and butter, delicious according to her, and the ginger biscuits to dip in tea, best bought at Fortnum and Mason. Most of all, though, she missed those endless walks in the green English parks, tidy and clean, trampling that carefully cut grass that almost creaked as one passed, producing a rhythmic sound.

'You do well to go there often and, as Dr Johnson said: when a man is tired of London, he's tired of life!' Then she added, 'Go, and when you come back, tell me all about it, let me know about the club. I'm glad they took you in, you'll see you'll be fine, the English are great people.' And again: 'I'm glad you're staying in Italy. Besides, how would you do without my advice?' Jicky laughed, amused.

Indeed, she would give her valuable suggestions on almost any subject. 'What do you say, Jicky, shall I go for the weekend away or should I save up?' Nicoletta would ask her. And then: 'Shall I buy that new dress?' Jicky urged her to go away, to buy the new dress, to never deprive herself of anything and to be happy. To not think too much about the future, but to live in the moment. The title of her painting exhibition, 'Seize the Fleeting Moment', could be the perfect life motto for her.

'Money has to be spent,' she advised, 'and then you're always working. Money has to be spent on something.'

Jicky instructed Nicoletta in many aspects of daily life. She never taught her how to decipher handwriting, though, or what the rules were. Never an explanation, not a word. 'Bring me the handwriting of the people you're interested in,' she would say. 'Have them write a few lines by hand on a sheet of paper and I'll know everything about them.' And so, they did. In great secrecy.

Then Jicky would go back to talking about her grandchildren, the neighbours who had gone to get her groceries from the shop in the square in Sirolo, the people in the small town and the visits she had received. Together with Nicoletta, she used to do her seasonal shopping by mail order. At that time, internet shopping was not yet in use, so Jicky received a mail-order catalogue from England with cashmere, cardigans, trousers and pullovers. Twice a year, in spring and autumn, she placed orders for her new wardrobe. She cared so much about the latest trends and fashion colours and, punctually, the parcels with the new garments would soon arrive in Sirolo.

Jicky began trying to change Nicoletta's English accent. It had to be pure British, sophisticated, the auxiliaries of verbs without too many contractions and sentences enriched with many adverbs. Absolutely no Americanised idioms. Jicky then went on to advise her to change her regular beach and later even tried to reshuffle her circle of friends. She succeeded with her pronunciation and with the beach, which absolutely had to be the one in Sirolo. Less so with friends.

'Jicky, I can't change my lifelong friends!' Nicoletta told her.

'They're not your equal, they don't have your depth, you mustn't lower yourself!' Jicky scolded her. Sometimes, she turned her nose up at the look or the way Nicoletta dressed. 'Do you walk around with that awful bag?' she would say, referring to a transparent plastic bag that Nicoletta used to take to the beach and which showed all the contents inside.

'Jicky, it's in fashion!' Nicoletta replied to her.

'It's ugly!' Jicky continued. 'Go to the little table, take that dark red leather clutch. It's a Hermès love letter holder, I had it made especially for me by Hermès, take it and don't let me see you with that ridiculous plastic container again, not even to go down to the beach.'

Jicky was like that. She could be so generous and selfless that you were left speechless. Who in the world could have given a Hermès bag if not her, simply because she was disturbed by the sight of a modern plastic accessory?

For Christmas 2005, Jicky had given Nicoletta a pen with a Victorian inkwell and a note: 'With love, Jicky.' Nicoletta, in turn, gave her books in English that she had bought in Rome and which she knew interested her. She had also found in Rome a bottle of her favourite Jicky perfume by Guerlain. It was almost unobtainable in those years, especially in the Marche, but also in Paris, since her son had not been able to buy her the special fragrance that she loved so much.

Chapter 13

Confession

Jicky gave Nicoletta an even greater gift in the years that followed. A revelation. One day, as she was telling her the story of when she was captured by the Nazis, she suddenly exclaimed: 'Do you know why they captured us and took us to prison?'

'Because there was the war, Jicky, and the Germans had occupied Paris,' Nicoletta answered her.

'Nico, do you know what I used to do?' Jicky asked her.

'Now I'll tell you. I was a British intelligence agent, operating in France undercover, sent by Churchill's government. I was carrying out very risky espionage operations, even though my speciality was handwriting expertise. I collaborated with our police, who brought me sheets of paper with handwritten lines and I had to tell them all the information that the handwriting revealed to me about the people under observation. I could pick up every secret, whether they were weak or strong, clever or tricky. Just everything. With this data, the other agents could then move around and make their decisions. It was considered a very important service. They would bring me pages and pages crammed with scriptures. Of women, men, officials, people of state, politicians and administrators. They would submit them to me. I would personally mingle among them, among these characters. And I would ask them to write a few lines by hand on a sheet of paper. I would know everything about their lives. What they kept jealously hidden. They no longer held any secrets for me. I have always studied, and graphic reading is a perfect science. No one can escape its rules. Not even if they try.

'A very useful work for espionage. It has always proved to be an infallible method. I have never misinterpreted it. It was always so simple and interesting to me. It was like reading the soul of a person you had never met before.

'I was one of the very few agents on duty at the time who was capable of such an activity. If you had not studied and were not properly prepared, you could never do it, you had to have the specialisation. I was also in charge of organising the Resistance units in France. I acted as a liaison with England. My partner carried out more conventional espionage operations. He recruited new contacts, distributed essential material to them.

'How did the Nazis find out about us? This we never understood. We were so guarded, many of my activities, I carried out from home, especially later, when the embassy closed. Then one day they came, the Nazis. They came for us knowing I was an agent of His Majesty. Someone betrayed me. I don't know who, though. We were very careful. We knew our lives were at risk.

'They interrogated us at length in the barracks. I denied it, then when I saw that they didn't believe me, I fell silent. I remained silent, I never revealed the names of the other agents. Nor that of the Resistance members. I never betrayed anyone. I didn't care to live knowing that I'd betrayed someone in my team and had caused some innocent person to lose their life because of me. To some of our collaborators who, like me, risked their lives and the lives of their loved ones.

'I never revealed anything. That's why they put me in that horrible prison. And I was pregnant. I thought I was going to die and to have the baby I was carrying die as well. I still can't believe that I could do it. That my son and I made it. All we had to endure in that cold cell.'

She finished the story in one breath, her voice jerky, convulsive, almost breathless, in apnoea. As fast as she could, as if she feared she would not be able to do it, to get to the end of her horrible story. Then silence fell. Jicky's eyes remained, as always, lost in the void, suffering. She never shed a tear. There was no hatred, nor desire for revenge. This time, perhaps, she felt lightened by the fact that she had been able to vent and to tell the truth as to why she had been caught. She was a British secret agent. Yes, that beautiful, cultured and refined woman had been an agent of the British intelligence, who later moved to Italy, more precisely to a small town of 4,000 residents, in the province of Ancona, and who led a normal-looking life.

She always recounted the horror of her capture, and how she had struggled to walk when she was rushed to the Gestapo Headquarters because she was wearing heels. She never, not even to her Nico, described what had happened in the cell during her days of captivity. Of the torture. She had only told her that, after being interrogated by the Gestapo, she had been grabbed by the arm and thrown to the floor of the freezing prison with no bed or blankets. Then the usual interminable silence.

She then revealed to Nicoletta the hiding place of her famous diaries. 'Open that drawer,' she confided to her.

'See that metal chest? Inside are my agendas, diaries and my phonebook. Many of my annual diaries were lost as a result of the moves I made, which were many. Perhaps they ended up in boxes packed and forgotten in some attic or warehouse. Others were picked up by some of my relatives during one of their visits and taken to Paris. Perhaps by my granddaughter. All these are the ones I managed to save and which I keep hidden here in this drawer, in the box that looks like a jewellery box.'

Nicoletta left the house that day with a thousand thoughts in her head. And a thousand questions. And a thousand secrets she would not reveal. Jicky had given her the honour of that burning confidence, leaving her scared. She had only seen spies and secret agents in action movies, American or British. She had heard about MI6, the CIA, Mossad, on television, or had read about them in the newspapers. She would never have imagined that one of her best friends was part of it. She could not even share the news with anyone. It could have been dangerous for her, too, if the story came out.

Surely Paolo knew about it? Even some of the older inhabitants from Sirolo. Certainly Dorothy. None of the friends who came to her house in the last years of her life knew. To them she confided events from the private sphere, some love of her youth, to each one something else, but without saying who she had really been many years before. She was a woman who kept her true secrets hidden in an inviolable chest, like the metal one that hid the diaries.

She had told Nicoletta everything with an open heart, not out of simple friendship. Although it certainly was not just because of that. She trusted her, yes, but it was because she wanted to leave the testimony of her great story to someone before it was erased forever by the passing of the years. And because, given her age, she feared that with the passing of time, her sacrifice and her heroic silence would be lost. She wanted to leave an indelible trace behind her. She was certainly not the type to write books about her history. She was different from Stella Rimington and the many other agents who told of their activities. Jicky could have given countless interviews, gone on national talk shows and become a celebrity. She had not wanted to do that, though. It was not her style.

Her oath of secrecy to the British government would last a lifetime. An invisible forever. But it is these invisible characters, along with people's knowledge and traditions that make history. Not just the famous ones. That is why the invisible are important to remember. And as the historian Professor Mario Maggi wrote:

> With the generation coming to an end, the heritage of unofficial culture and experience ceases to be a living reality. The knowledge of the people appears in the genuine nature of the people who inhabited our land. For these reasons, we have been investigating the popular traditions of our native country for years... It is the memory, the soul of a people, that we want to pass on, and along with it, the interest in our very often forgotten traditions. We wanted to pass on to the young and the not-so-young documentary sources, which would otherwise have been lost, concerning our origins and the behaviour of so many people of the past, who, for various reasons, have left their distinguishing mark. With our writings, we also hope to leave, *intra et extra moenia*, a good memory of those of us who have dedicated part of our free time to the research of our cultural and historical heritage.[25]

Chapter 14

The King's White Horse

'On its way into town, the king's white horse turned into a donkey,' is an Indian proverb that sums up a basic concept. Everything can change. A white horse can suddenly turn into a donkey on a journey.

Paolo had always been very affectionate with Jicky. Attentive and caring, he was also very tolerant. He always let her go when she had to make a trip to London or elsewhere. He always left her hands free and allowed her maximum independence. A perfect companion. Thanks to her, however, Paolo had the opportunity to live in one of Sirolo's most elegant residences, meet with influential, high-level personalities: artists, fashion designers, antique dealers, entrepreneurs and well-known professionals. From all over the world. In addition, he benefited from the constant cultural stimuli of a woman of Jicky's stature.

At one point, Paolo fell ill and needed dialysis twice a week. He was still young, but life had condemned him to this slavery. He began to stay in Ancona more and more often, going to the hospital for dialysis and then staying in the Marche capital, Ancona, for longer and longer periods. Jicky was worried about the disease, but at the same time relieved because her companion was in the expert hands of the doctors at the dialysis centre. In those years, many printers, such as Paolo, touched the ink with their bare hands and did not wear gloves. Black ink was mainly made with carbon, while coloured inks often contained heavy metals such as chromium, cadmium and lead, which are now known to be toxic. Metal pigments and petroleum-based solvents posed serious health risks for printers. They were simply advised to drink a glass of milk to detoxify in the evening once at home. This is why many of them became seriously ill.

However, Paolo started spending more and more time in Ancona. He stayed out all day, and even went there on days not scheduled for dialysis. He only went back to Jicky's in Sirolo to sleep. She was not alarmed, though, believing his new habits were related to his weak health. Then the worst happened. When buying the beautiful house in Sirolo, bought using money from the sale of the flat she owned in Paris, Jicky had made a mistake that would prove fatal. She had registered the new house to Paolo, probably to streamline bureaucratic procedures, as she had neither Italian nationality nor residence in Sirolo. She must have thought that the notary's deed for the purchase of the property would proceed more quickly, given the haste with which she wanted to conclude the deal. It was the biggest mistake of her life. At that very moment, the king's white horse turned into a donkey. No longer a noble thoroughbred, but a common pack-horse.

One day, out of the blue, Paolo came home from Ancona with a document. He was in a hurry to show it to her. It was a deed of sale for the property. Paolo had sold the house without Jicky's approval, even though she was the real 'owner', since the money used to buy it was all hers. Paolo was formally only the owner on paper. The deed of sale contained a clause, though, which offered some kind of protection. Jicky could stay in the house until her death, and in the meantime would receive a little sum of money with the proceeds of the sale. The total amount was around £10,000; a relatively paltry sum for a big, two-storey house, the most historic in Sirolo, located right in the centre of town. Was the money purely given to Jicky to ease Paolo's conscience?

Paolo had bought a flat in Ancona with the money, also behind Jicky's back, who had been left completely in the dark. When Paolo showed her the sales contract, Jicky almost fainted. How could he have hatched such a plan with the money she had earned in Paris? It was an affront, disrespectful, and worse still, a scam.

Then came the final blow. Paolo had not just been going to Ancona for his weekly dialysis; he had met a lady of his age in the city whom he would shortly marry. The couple would live in the flat they had bought with Jicky's money. Paolo's new wife was a seamstress in a garment and clothing company. A good, simple, local lady. Short and very normal. Nothing to do with Jicky's histrionic and eclectic personality.

In all this tsunami, Jicky's son Claude learned of his mother's house, which was, in fact, no longer there. Gone in a flash. He became very angry with her and did not speak to her again for some time, blaming her and, in fact, making her suffer even more. Many, including Nicoletta, wondered in amazement how a woman as witty as she was, with her history as a secret agent, could have been fooled in this way by a simple village man like Paolo.

It is well known that secret agents are trained from the very beginning to master their emotions, to control their passions, not to become too attached to anyone, to be cold and rational, and sometimes even to be cynical and calculating. So how could this have happened? The explanation is easy. She was naive because she loved him deeply and would have made any sacrifice for him, would have sacrificed her life for his sake, would have allowed him everything. She could never have hated him.

If you think about it, a secret service agent is trained to sacrifice themselves. To deny themselves for a good cause, for the government, for Britain. Even to the point of losing their own life. It is a process of annihilation that they undertake. Perhaps it is instilled in them after they are drafted, during training. Back then, the reason they undertook such work was mostly out of a spirit of sacrifice. If death occurred while on duty, then it was for the greater good. No regrets.

Jicky had done this for Paolo, out of love, as she had done it in the past for her country. Always out of love. Her son did not understand that his mother was simply tricked by the man she loved and harboured a kind of hatred towards her that was destined to last for a long time. Claude did not realise that it was not a targeted action against him.

A greater love for her companion to his detriment, to the detriment of her son, of that sole heir born in one of the hardest moments of her life. Claude, at this point, could not help but be jealous and think about his lost inheritance. Hurt, he distanced himself from his mother. He did not comfort her for being cheated by Paolo, her great love.

Jicky accepted the situation, despite herself. She was not resigned. She understood. She did not hate Paolo and had no anger towards him. She had never seen him as the king's white horse that had turned into a donkey on the way to the city. 'Paolo was ill, very ill,' Jicky said, years later. 'He must have felt lost and insecure. He wanted to find a nurse, someone who could assist him if the situation got worse, if his health deteriorated. A sick person should never be judged. You cannot know what goes on in his head, a thousand anxieties, a thousand frailties. With that woman there was no passion, no love. She was just a support for him, almost like a carer.'

These were the remarks Jicky made when someone jumped in and took the opportunity to attack Paolo for that despicable gesture. No one could judge Paolo. She did not, so no one else could. Was he the love of her life? Jicky no longer knew. She did not even know anymore if she had done the right thing in leaving her husband in Paris and to live on nothing but passion and love that would lead her to similar results.

It is a fact that Paolo passed away many years before her, despite the great age difference between the pair, and even though people in Sirolo had always mocked him by saying that he lived with his mother. Paolo died suddenly and no one had the delicacy to inform her. 'One day I was walking my dogs,' Jicky later recounted. 'I stopped in front of the walls of Sirolo. There was a sign for a funeral. I got closer and read a death notice. It was a bit worn; it had been there for several days. It said: Paolo Paolini.'

Here, Jicky was moved and then started to tell the story again:

I thought I had read it wrong. Yes, it did say that Paolo, my Paolo, had died and that the funeral had already taken place a few days earlier. I feel sick at that announcement. I was about to faint. I ran home distraught. How could it have happened that no one had told me? Not even my closest friends. How could they be so cruel? What an absence of sensitivity. It took me a long time to recover. I couldn't even say one last goodbye to him, pay my respects, bid him farewell.

Then Jicky stopped abruptly, moved. She no longer felt like talking. She was reliving that pain as if it had happened in that instant. It was likely that her friends in Sirolo had not informed her about the funeral because they were embarrassed by the presence of his official wife, his new family, at the ceremony. Jicky would never have created an awkward situation. She would never have passed herself off as Paolo's true companion. She would simply have wanted to be in a hidden corner at the back of the church to say goodbye to her great love. To send him one last kiss and, mingling with the crowd, be able to leave a flower on his coffin. A caress to the soul.

Chapter 15

The Seven Lives

'Can you see in Rome if you can find some books on the history of ancient Rome in English?' Jicky asked Nicoletta one Saturday afternoon. 'I've noticed that I've a few gaps and I want to read up on that topic. I want to go deeper. 'I've started taking Russian lessons,' she continued. 'It's a difficult language but I'm studying. A teacher is coming and I'm working hard.'

This was the best reaction she could have had to a fate that had relegated her, for the first time in her life, to the mercy of loneliness. She found comfort in culture, in studying a new language, and was satisfied with the progress she was able to achieve. She began to speak Russian, proudly showing her notebooks with Cyrillic writing. She began again. A new life to fill. And so, she turned her house into a cultural salon. It became a bustle of people. Her friend Dorothy, professors Sandra and Giorgio from Bologna, English holidaymakers and antique dealers. The more she complained about being almost always alone in the house, the more people of all kinds would come to visit. It was always full. Even Nicoletta did not leave her alone, calling her every day and visiting her whenever she returned from Rome. She even spent Christmas and Easter afternoons with her.

When Nicoletta went to the Rome editorial room of BBC Radio to give interviews in English about current Italian political events, Jicky exclaimed: 'You see, if you're called to the BBC it is thanks to me! It's thanks to me that you speak that elegant English, untainted by other accents, without my teaching you would never have been asked by the BBC!'

Jicky managed to cope well with the loss of Paolo and decided she wanted to spend the rest of her days in Sirolo. To never return to live in Paris or London again. With the contract Paolo had given her, she could stay in that house forever. And as General de Gaulle declared on 18 June 1940: 'Is defeat final? No!... The flame of the French Resistance must not be extinguished and will not be extinguished.' Even for Jicky, defeat was never final, and it had led her to continuous periods of resistance throughout her life.

'Nico, why do all your friends want to meet me? I'm glad you bring them to me, but I don't understand what they find interesting in an old, English lady,' Jicky asked Nicoletta smugly one day.

'Jicky, they always hear about you,' she replied. 'I tell them about the nice things you've done, the interesting people you've met, about Hermès, and your calligraphic expertise. Everyone wants to have their handwriting analysed by you. They want to meet you, you intrigue them.'

'Bring them along, I'm happy to speak to them,' said Jicky, nodding. 'But don't bring me any more people like that New Zealander you met in London who works in Ancona. What was the name of the yacht captain, that engineer? Ah yes, David. I didn't like him at all from the start. I didn't give him a graphic analysis either, mind you. He behaved badly when he came. Maybe you didn't notice, while I was showing him my house and period furniture. He bent over my precious Persian carpet, turned one corner upside down to check if it was authentic or not. A real boor. A rude one.'

'I'm sorry, Jicky. He won't be coming around here anymore. He just wanted to see Sirolo. He didn't have his car and I gave him a lift,' Nicoletta said as she tried to justify herself to the offended Jicky.

'For the rest, bring whoever you want,' continued Jicky. 'My house is open to all your friends and the nicest ones, I will ask them to write a few lines by hand on a sheet of paper, so I will know everything about them and reveal it to you,' she winked complicitly.

She was happy to have so many people around her, since she no longer had any family of her own, especially knowing that so many young people wanted to meet her. She had become a myth for all the people who had heard of her. As well as the marshal of the local carabinieri, everyone had wanted to meet her: the owner of an insurance company in Sirolo; a policeman from Osimo who worked in Milan; an important diplomat from the American embassy in Rome who was visiting the Conero Riviera. Like moths to a flame, they all wanted to visit the house of that eccentric English lady.

Jicky was ready to show every corner of her house to her visitors: the old paintings, the various furnishings and period furniture, almost as if it were a museum. She recounted its origins and memories. She barely had time to rest from her troubles and embark on a new life, when another bombshell suddenly landed at her feet. It manifested itself in the form of a letter. From Paris this time. It was from her favourite granddaughter, a missive full of hatred and resentment.

She wrote that she did not respect her, that she was a bad grandmother, and that she wanted to express all her contempt and disdain for her. She told her that she wished she had a grandmother like all the others. In black and white, it was a detailed letter full of resentment and anger addressed to an old lady, her grandmother, who lived alone in another country, without the support of her son. It was the final straw.

This time, Jicky reacted very badly. She was distraught and cried for days. A strong 1,000-year-old oak tree had crumbled in an instant. In half an instant. The condemnation of her granddaughter really broke her down. Then the reaction. Hard as ever. This time even more so. She had to fight back against the blow she had suffered. To the devastating pain she had had to endure.

From that letter onwards, Jicky was never the same. Out of the blue, she made all the photographs of her granddaughter disappear. They had been scattered all over the house, on the bedside table in the bedroom, on the living room table, on the shelves in the other rooms. All disposed of. From that moment on, her granddaughter was as good as dead to her. She no longer existed. She would never mention her again, not even before she died. She had processed the devastating loss, the mourning, and, with a flick of the wrist, had erased her from her life once and for all.

***

Jicky was now very old. Still lucid and witty, but the aches and pains of age were beginning to set in. She was often surrounded by the usual people who visited her, brought her groceries home, and who dropped by to say hello. Jicky was not so lonely. She had by her side all the objects of a life that represented her memories, the people she had loved. She was always in telephone contact with Charles, her first love, who called her from America on Valentine's Day and birthdays. She felt, however, that the end was approaching. What was the point of living any longer at this point?

'Nico, how will you manage without me when I go where I have to go?' she asked, worriedly. She could no longer advise her, warn her against those who wanted to harm her, protect her from the many pitfalls.

She lived to the end with strength and dignity. Her friend Sandra dedicated a poem to her, a tribute to that mysterious and haughty Englishwoman:

> To Jicky
> My dear friend
> Tall and proud woman,
> cultured and mysterious,
> daughter of an empire
> now dissolved.
> You have been to France,
> mother and partisan
> wife, on an enchanted island
> Conquered

From a young love
In Italy you stayed.
In the white country by the sea,
between books and writing with
beloved animals
you entrusted your dreams
to the wings of birds
through the window
from the big old house,
the last of your long life.[26]

***

Slowly, Jicky left, almost on tiptoe. She realised this when one evening, in order to close a window that had blown open by the wind, she fell and could no longer get up. She stayed all night begging for help, cold, stuck to the floor of the room that had turned to ice. No one heard her. Her body had betrayed her. She was almost 97 years old.

From that terrible experience onwards, she spent more and more time in bed. She was afraid of getting out and falling again. She hired a carer who fed her and helped her wash. Eventually, she was no longer hungry and fed herself with a straw. She was always in bed and got bedsores, the excruciating pain tormenting her every time she moved. She complained for days on end. She did not want to go to hospital, though, preferring instead to spend the last days of her life in that house overflowing with happy memories. Of her love with Paolo. Of the paintings of the great Parisian painters. Of her family's heirlooms.

Jicky died on 22 January 2011, at the age of 97. All her closest friends flocked to her funeral. Nicoletta braved the ice on the Gran Sasso Mountain and returned from Rome by car. There were also people there from Sirolo who had known her for years, about ten in all. Missing from the funeral that day were her son and grandchildren.

None of them was present in the church of San Nicola in Sirolo. They had not left Paris.

At the entrance to the cemetery walls, set among the stones of the Conero, is an inscription:

> The view of the tombs
> inspires citizens
> with the memory
> of the brevity of life,
> the harmony of minds
> in serene profitable work
> for the greater good
> of all.

Jicky would be buried as requested in her last will and testament. In a tomb like those painted by the Pre-Raphaelites. On the bare ground of the cemetery there would be a white marble headstone, simple, not at all lavish:

Jicky Juvénal
7 November 1913 – 22 January 2011.

An icy rain mixed with the tears of those present who could not stop crying. No one was surprised by her son's absence. He had not come to see her even when he had been told that Jicky was dying. He did not arrive in Sirolo until a month after the funeral, to collect some personal belongings. Someone said they finally saw him shed a tear as he was about to leave for Paris.

A few years after the death of his mother, in June 2016, at the age of 72, Claude died in Paris, suddenly, following a stroke.

***

At the writing of this biography, the British government has never awarded Jicky/Hazel Juvénal-Smith any honour, certificate of gratitude or commendation for her enormous courage and service to the nation, or for the sacrifice she offered. Not even a posthumous honour. No one has ever paid tribute to her figure and contribution. There is no medal for valour or plaque. No one has ever celebrated her deeds. No State visit to her grave in Sirolo. In 2022 a plaque was attached to the wall of her former house by the Sirolo Cultural Circle (see Part 3). Perhaps this is because Jicky was not included in the official intelligence lists of the British government. Or because she escaped them. Invisible in life, a spook, a spectre as they call them at MI6, those agents on the secret lists, hidden in embassies and consulates. Invisible when dead, hidden in the cemetery of a pleasant, small town on the Marche Riviera.

Her suffering and torture had been the same, however, as the agents on the official SOE lists. Those who rightly received honours, medals and recognition later.

After calling the advisors of the British government's National Archives for help on finding documentation on those secret agents who operated during the Second World War, the answer was that apart from those names on the official lists, there are others secreted in government files. Unfortunately, however, other names have been lost.

Jicky was one of Churchill's Angels. That group of women sent by the British premier to the front line in Nazi-occupied territories. People like Jicky have sacrificed themselves through their service to ensure our freedom today.

As Commander-in-Chief of the First Aid Nursing Yeomanry (FANY), patroness of the Special Forces Club and daughter of Queen Elizabeth II, The Princess Royal describes these women in the introduction to the book *The Women Who Spied for Britain* as follows: 'None of these brave women aspired to be heroes but without them the

Resistance movements in France, and across the continent, would not have been as successful as they were, and we owe them all a huge debt of gratitude.'[27]

The people who frequented Jicky's house on the Conero in her last years of life were unaware of the real work she performed for the British government. Everything remained secret.

Although Jicky died in Sirolo in 2011, perhaps the first time she had lost her life was in Paris, many years before. When unfeeling Nazis had tried to tear her soul away. Torturing her in a cold prison while she was pregnant. They had not succeeded. She had resisted and was reborn to new life, stronger than before. No doubt she is now somewhere in heaven trying to read someone's handwriting.

Some people swear that they hid the bottle of her favourite perfume, Jicky, inside the coffin before it was sealed forever.

PART TWO

The French Resistance: An In-Depth Investigation Using Jicky's Connections

Chapter 1

The Resistance: Imagine Spring!

'Imagine spring.' Yes, 'think of spring!'

This was the wish the students exchanged at Christmas in Paris during the German occupation. Even though they themselves, with their youth, were the real spring. They were by now used to seeing their friends and relatives being shot, the tree trunks consumed by the enormous number of bullets, coloured red by the blood of people they loved. Or perhaps they knew of people who had been executed without trial by summary German justice. People who were merely suspects. Despite the oppression, there were still people intent on organising resistance operations.

They knew the hunger. Food was rationed and people very often skipped meals. They knew the cold. There was a shortage of wood and the long, freezing winters were difficult to get through. Imagine spring!

They knew the curfew. One could not go out between 5 pm and 5 am. Shut in the house, people were accompanied by the multiple sounds of gunfire at all times. It was impossible to doze off for a few hours at night. Fear, hunger and cold hardly left time for respite. It was exhausting. Those who had family members in the 'Free Zone' of Vichy, under the command of the French Nazi collaborator Marshal Pétain, had to apply for a proper visa just to visit. People obeyed, but, 'imagine spring!'

Also executed were those who collaborated on the production and distribution of the *Journal des Volontaires*, the newspaper of the Maquis, those Resistance fighters hiding in the bush in the hills. The centre of the Resistance was in the Vercors Massif, in the French Prealps, in the scrubland of eastern France. Here, in 1944, they were decimated by

German forces assisted by the French militia. The Vercors scrubland thus became the symbol of the French Resistance. They gave themselves courage by singing '*Le Chant des Partisans*', the song of the partisans, which includes the lyrics, 'Friend, do you hear the black flight of crows over our plains..?', 'It is we who break the prison bars for our brothers/ The hatred at our heels and hunger that drives us...' 'Friend, if you fall, a friend emerges from the shadows in your place...' or 'In the night freedom listens to us...'

Forty pages of the *Journal des Volontaires* were printed every week. Stencils were used for the pictures, just as Banksy and other street artists do in their murals today. Articles were written and printed on Roneo machines.

Many of the hundreds of underground newspapers were finely printed, despite paper rationing and harsh repression. Those caught with newspapers were shot or deported to concentration camps. In addition to newspapers, false identity papers were also printed. Although the SOE provided false identity cards for their agents, members of the French Resistance stole blank cards and attached photographs and used fake stamps.

Everything was done in secret from safe hiding places in wartime France. It was vital to keep thinking about spring. The memory of a ray of sunshine, of the blossoming of nature. A few sprigs of a romantic peach blossom. The yellow of the mimosa, the sharp scent of the lily of the valley. The strength of the wild broom plant, the flower favoured by the poet Giacomo Leopardi for its tenacity. A little flower of blinding yellow, fragile in appearance, which in reality is able to withstand both wind and lack of rain.

Here, the thought of spring, understood not as a period of time but as a state of mind, was the only thing left to keep the flame of survival burning. To stay alive and well, and not just to exist. What better wish could be exchanged at Christmas than the desire to remain anchored in existence. 'Lend yourself to others, but give yourself to yourself,' as Montaigne wrote in his essays.

A walk in nature, with its rhythms, which never changes and cyclically re-blooms, is the only model to rely on in order not to succumb to death and sadness. To react, one had to think in a spring-like way. Hold high the banner of hope. Hope. What an inappropriate term in those years of pain and frustration. Of overall imprisonment. Even for students forced to stay at home and listen to the roar of the planes. Watching their contrails in the skies, trying to imagine, following their directions, which areas would be bombed. Identifying with the people under the bombs. Only imagination could save them from madness. Only spring gave them a semblance of a future.

Many students enjoyed putting stickers with the letter V for Victory in the Paris subway and metro cars. The idea had been imported from Britain, which had spread the concept of victory to raise spirits. Only with that in mind could one return to battle. In Morse code, victory is spelled like this: ... –. Three dots and a dash. In Beethoven's Fifth (Vth) Symphony, the rhythmic pattern corresponds to the Morse code for the letter V, for victory. How ironic that a German musical score became the anthem of British troops during the bombing of England. Beethoven had himself been a symbol of resistance against dictatorship, when in 1804 he had distanced himself from Napoleon, who had proclaimed himself Emperor of France.

Winston Churchill's famous sign, V for Victory, was made with the index and middle finger in the shape of a V. 'The V sign is the symbol of the unconquerable will of the occupied territories, and a portent of the fate awaiting the Nazi tyranny,' thundered the British premier.

The Nazis found these Vs everywhere on the Paris metro and pretended they had invented them so as not to give satisfaction to the general public. But the word for victory in German is Sieg. The falsehood was hard to swallow, although in *Mein Kampf*, Hitler had already explained how something untrue, if repeated many times, could become reality.

Hitler mocked Churchill because of his age, referring to him as an old man. He even called him Mister in his speeches to ridicule him. This was quite natural for a champion of all discriminations like Hitler, although calling someone old was nothing when compared to what he did to others. Jews, children with Down's syndrome, the handicapped and homosexuals.

Life was very hard for those French intellectuals and thinkers imprisoned in their homes, who thought of themselves as 'prisoners'. In his work *The Plague*, which is a metaphor for the Nazi occupation of France, the writer and philosopher Albert Camus repeated the word prisoner and prison multiple times. Camus also contributed to another Resistance daily newspaper, *Combat*, and his editorial celebrating the joy of liberation is famous. 'The greatness of man,' he wrote, 'lies in his decision to be stronger than his condition.'

In *The Plague* Camus perfectly described the state of mind of those under Nazi occupation. The separation from their loved ones. Living one day with terror in their soul, the next with a lighter spirit. The not remembering, sometimes, the features of the faces of loved ones because of the distance between them. Camus examined feelings in depth. He spoke of husbands and lovers who, because of their distance, found themselves jealous. Of children who had lived with their mother by barely looking at her, now trying to recall every crease in her face with regret. Of doubled sufferings, both their own and those they imagined in their absent loved ones, child, spouse or lover. Of idle people in their towns, abandoned 'to the deceptive games of memory.'[28]

They strolled aimlessly in the same streets where they once strolled with the absent. The first misfortune caused by the plague/war was exile. The feeling of it and the emptiness people carried inside themselves constantly. The unreasonable desire to go back in time or instead to hasten it. The expectation but then the acceptance that that person was no longer present. One had to come to terms with time. There was resignation in one's condition as a prisoner. And those who wanted to live in the future quickly renounced it, 'as far as possible, suffering the wounds that the imagination eventually inflicts on those who trust it.'[29]

People had lost the habit of calculating the duration of their separation. In order not to suffer, many tried not to think about the day of liberation, 'to no longer look towards the future and to always, shall we say, keep their eyes down.'[30] No longer thinking of the future, they lived with a memory that served no purpose. 'Impatient of their present, hostile for their own past and deprived of a future, they resembled those people who are confined behind bars by justice.'[31]

And as exiles at home or exiled far away, these people could do nothing but cling to fantasy and imagination to keep from going mad.

The virus, which Camus disguised as the plague but which is always that horrible war, was always lurking. An evil that man always carries within him, ready to awaken again in the future.

> ...Rieux remembered that this cheerfulness was always threatened: he knew what the crowd ignored, and what one can read in books, namely, that the plague bacillus never dies or disappears, that it can remain for tens of years asleep in furniture and linen, that it waits patiently in rooms, cellars, suitcases, handkerchiefs and wrappings, and that perhaps the day would come when, by misfortune and teaching men, the plague would awaken its rats to send them to die in a happy city.[32]

Another important text to read to understand occupied France is the book by the professor and literary scholar Jean Guéhenno, *Journal des années noires, 1940-1944* (*The Diary of the Dark Years, 1940-1944*)[33] published in France in 1947. The book is fundamental in analysing the gloomy situation in France on a day-to-day basis, and Guéhenno's daily notes in his diaries are a great documentary source.

Like Camus, Guéhenno also made frequent use of the word 'prisoner'. Prisoner and prisoners for him are the intellectuals and thinkers. He was a high school (lyceum) teacher who lost contact with his students, and the climate of suspicion that spread even in schools made him feel ill. His greatest suffering, however, was that, as an intellectual, he did not collaborate in the French Resistance, did not risk his life like the Resistance fighters. Those who, captured and taken to their death in train carriages, with the knowledge of the end close at hand, chanted the 'La Marseillaise'. Not even like the young British and Americans who went to war to liberate the French, who were so incapable of defending their borders. Just remember the Maginot Line, that 'impenetrable wall' built to protect the French border from a possible German attack. Instead, Hitler's army simply moved to the north in order to invade, only for France, with its weak army, to surrender just over a month later. The armistice that followed was a betrayal of the French, and de Gaulle fled to London to lead the French Resistance.

Guéhenno saw the yellow signs lit up in the underground station posted by the Nazis to announce an imminent execution and his heart broke. He and his culture were sheltered. He attacked the French who did not fight, calling them cowards. He called the Nazis rats. All alike in their grey uniforms, they were like automatons because of their expressionless gaze and obedience to superior orders.

He suffered further when, in 1942, many of the statues in Paris were torn down by the Nazis for their metal, which they needed in their own metallurgical industries. They knocked down the image of any important historical figure, any symbol, to make a weapon or the barrel of a cannon.

Guéhenno was annoyed by Hitler's speeches and paid homage to Churchill's. He was furious with French collaborators like Marshal Pétain. At 84 years of age, he was so full of himself that on the 1 May, Labour Day, he also celebrated the holiday dedicated to his namesake, Saint Phillip. Guéhenno also mocked Pétain for his statements such as: 'I give to France myself'. 'Keep the gift,' Guéhenno commented. He also rebuked Pétain for his eagerness to appear in full health at 84 for fear of being replaced by someone else as head of the Vichy government, as indeed happened two years later, in 1942, with Prime Minister Pierre Laval. In reality, Pétain's venerable age saved him from being executed at the end of the war, like many of Hitler's friendly collaborators.

Guéhenno found his own concept of spring in the great thinkers and philosophers and their views. In Rousseau, Pascal, Voltaire, Montesquieu, Montaigne, Nietzsche and Michelet. Between ups and downs, he worked on a book about his favourite philosopher, Jean-Jacques Rousseau. He wrote his powerful diary about life during the occupation, a valuable source of historical reality, even though he sometimes disguised the names of the protagonists to avoid possible Nazi repercussions. He kept in mind all of Hitler's speeches, and those of Churchill, which he listened to secretly via the BBC on his radio. After all, listening to the BBC was a punishable offence in occupied Europe.

Guéhenno could not fail to notice the seemingly nonsensical phrases launched by the BBC that were nothing more than coded messages for British secret agents infiltrating France, i.e., the SOE's F and RF Sections. Sometimes simple musical messages, they used Beethoven's Fifth, or V spelled with a Roman numeral, for example, as part of the V for Victory. This meant that D-Day was approaching in all its triumph.

Diaries, often considered inferior literary works, are instead fundamental in reconstructing the moods and feelings of certain historical periods. Jicky's famous diaries are the same, even if they post-date the Second World War.

Chapter 2

Bernard Buffet, the Expressionist Painter

An interesting character to analyse in order to understand the dark period of the occupation in France is the expressionist painter Bernard Buffet, not least because he became a close friend of Jicky. It is not known exactly when – whether during or after the war – and on what occasion they met. Buffet mixed in the same cultural circles as Jicky, and the literary cafés they visited, such as the Café Flore, which were also frequented by Sartre and Camus, became famous after the war.

Buffet was a teenager when Paris was occupied, and he experienced the bombings and the horrors of war with great suffering. He came from a modest family. As a child, his mother took him to the Louvre Museum on Sundays to admire the paintings of the great masters. During the occupation, however, the Louvre was deprived of its great masterpieces, after they were carefully packed by the museum curators at night and transported in small trucks, sometimes even in cars, to the châteaux of the Loire or other secret hiding places to protect them from theft by the Nazis, who were notoriously greedy for works of art, with Göring being the worst offender.

First and foremost to be saved was Leonardo da Vinci's 'Mona Lisa'. Perfectly packaged, it was taken away by the curators as if it were a flesh-and-blood queen to be protected. Constantly threatened by the Nazi hierarchs who wanted to get their hands on the great masterpieces, the courageous men and women of the Louvre managed to get them to safety. One curator even took the 'Mona Lisa' to the room where she slept, risking her life for this priceless painting.

The various vicissitudes of the Louvre curators to save their works of art are well described in Gerri Chanel's book, *Saving Mona Lisa: The Battle to Protect the Louvre and its Treasures from the Nazis*,[34] while Bernard O'Connor's *Operation Ebensburg*[35] tells the story of how SOE's Austrian 'Bonzos' rescued looted European art.

At the time of the occupation of Paris, Bernard Buffet was just a sensitive boy, frightened by the horrors of the Nazi war. Where did he find his spring hope? In art and painting. Upset by the violence and daily crimes, he poured all his fear into painting. Pencils, brushes and canvases were his best companions. He enrolled in an art school, which he attended regularly every afternoon, where he drew maniacally and bulimically. He fed on the great classics, the ones he had seen as a child when his mother took him to the Louvre on weekends. He studied art at the Lycée Carnot and from 1943-45 studied at the École des Beaux-Arts in Paris. He became a precocious talent. At only 20 years old, he received the highest accolade from French academic critics and was the new hope for French art. His name appeared next to Picasso's for the first time, with art critics claiming that he would be his successor.

He drew sad and suffering faces, bent trees and landscapes with impeccable technique. However, the suffering that accompanied him during the war years can be seen in all his work. The colour scale is almost always in shades of grey, like his state of mind. His painting 'Horror of War' aroused great interest. It showed bare bodies, thin and suffering, thrown to the ground. Many likened it to Picasso's 'Guernica', and Buffet's representation of war, like Picasso, was always very topical.

Together with other, mostly young, painters, Buffet formed L'Homme Témoin (The Witness) group in 1948, which promoted a style of expressive social realism in opposition to the prevailing taste for abstractionism. According to their manifesto drafted by the critic Bouret, 'painting exists to bear witness and nothing human can remain outside of it.'

Their paintings portrayed everyday life in a bleak and pessimistic manner. Haftmann described their work as 'the pictorial equivalent of existentialism' and said that 'what these painters bore witness to was the emptiness of the world, the desolation of things abandoned in the spectral sterility of space, the vulnerability of man.' The desperate attitude was very much in vogue at the time and the group's works, especially those of Buffet, proved very popular with collectors.[36]

Buffet painted in his dark little flat in Paris, even placing his canvases in the bathroom. Every day he worked obsessively on forty, fifty pieces. Without stopping, without sleeping. For him, drawing was the only way to feel good. Yet he was unaware of his talent. He drew on canvas with a sure hand without ever making preparatory sketches and had an impeccable technique due to exhausting studies.

After the war, gallery owners competed for his work. A great Hollywood director and producer, Jean Negulesco, when travelling to Paris, fell in love with Buffet's paintings and bought dozens of them, taking them back as gifts to American film stars. In the 1953 film, *How to Marry a Millionaire*, with Marilyn Monroe and Lauren Bacall, one of the girls tries to sell a valuable painting to get rich. It was a painting by Bernard Buffet.

Humphrey Bogart and Lauren Bacall bought a Buffet painting on a romantic trip to Paris as a souvenir and a reminder of their love. Sophia Loren even has a sketchy portrait of Bernard Buffet that she keeps in her home under a small Picasso painting. The Bernard Buffet phenomenon was almost on a par with what happened with The Beatles years later. Picasso tried to snub the young Buffet. He did not want to consider him as his heir, despite several comparisons made by leading art critics of the time. Witnesses told of Picasso entering an influential gallery in Paris where a painting by Buffet was hanging, along with others by several important artists. He remained there for three minutes, glued to Buffet's painting. He became irritated whenever some of his friends sang Buffet's praises, including the poet, playwright, and writer Jean Cocteau.

Others told how one Sunday, while Picasso was having lunch with his children Claude and Paloma, they caught a glimpse of Bernard Buffet at a nearby table. Claude and Paloma jumped up and went to ask the young painter for an autograph. Picasso, meanwhile, was unable to hide his irritation and jealousy at such a gesture.[37]

Bernard Buffet's fame remained immense throughout the 1950s, when he became close friends with Jicky in Paris. The bars, bistros and cafés of Paris where Jicky and Buffet met acted as cultural incubators, but never so prominently as in Saint-Germain-des-Prés after the war.[38] It was an extraordinary concentration of great talents who were together in an area of Paris almost 2 kilometres wide. From morning to night, these great thinkers met to exchange their innovative ideas, to write and to discuss. These meeting places had almost a family atmosphere that favoured the circulation of the most innovative theories.

Sartre wrote that 'people would come in and find that they all knew each other, each person was privy to every detail of his neighbour's private life, but one didn't bother to say, "good morning", although they did so immediately if they met somewhere else.' Before 1944, Sartre only worked at Café Flore three hours in the morning and three hours in the evening.

Jicky knew them all, of course, but she was very close to Bernard Buffet. What is more, Buffet cohabited for a time with another friend of Jicky's, Pierre Bergé, who later became the historical partner of Yves Saint Laurent. For several years before this, however, Bergé had been the faithful companion/boyfriend of Bernard Buffet. The two lived together in a small villa in Provence, after Buffet's brief marriage to a girl had ended in a quick divorce. Bergé had helped Buffet with his skill as a writer, but above all with his copious connections in the aristocratic, political and cultural elite. At the time, it was rumoured that Bergé was the occult prompter of government men in the 1950s. Jicky, well-connected in that world thanks to her marriage to the Hermés scion, was Bergé's confidante.

Jicky had always assiduously frequented that world of French intellectuals who met in Parisian literary cafés. Buffet and Bergé knew the likes of the writer Georges Simenon, who loved to write on the island of Porquerolles, where Jicky and her husband owned a luxurious hotel.

Even after the split between Buffet and Bergé (a French gallerist declared at the time that Buffet was the genius and Bergé the materialist), Jicky remained Bergé's friend when he started dating Yves Saint Laurent. And with Saint Laurent, too, a solid bond began.

Bernard Buffet's fame began to fade as a result of poor communication choices. He suddenly became rich and began to flaunt the riches he had acquired by selling his paintings. He bought a beautiful Rolls-Royce and had himself photographed in it by the French tabloids, receiving fierce criticism from all quarters. Back then, secrecy was synonymous with depth and talent. His purchase of a chateau where he lived with Bergé also did not go unnoticed and was criticised.

Today, a painter who associates with fashion designers or jet-set personalities is considered fashionable. In those days, an artist who was a socialite, a frequenter of fashionable parties and jet-setters was considered very negatively. Especially if he also liked to be photographed and appeared on tabloid covers. Picasso never made such a mistake, always remaining an intellectual and committed painter. Such levity was fatal for Buffet, who antagonised the austere world of art critics, who suddenly began to distance themselves from him.

Jicky was always fond of Buffet and his works. His paintings were proudly displayed in her home in Sirolo. Indeed, his painting of Venice remained in her room next to her bed for almost fifty years until her death.

Bernard Buffet painted all his life, but the bitterness born in the years of the Nazi occupation always lingered in his heart and was expressed in all his drawings and paintings. Despair was always lurking. Until that very sad day when he began to feel a tremor in his hands. Diagnosed with Parkinson's disease, he realised that he would no longer be able to paint. He had survived the war by painting. He had fed himself on art all his life. Painting was the purpose of his existence. Thanks to painting, in the 1940s he had managed to see that spring light at the end of the tunnel and survive. Now it was gone.

On 4 October 1999, after a walk and lunch, he told his wife he would go and rest before resuming painting. They found him, hours later, on the ground, with a plastic bag around his neck. He had decided to end his existence and had suffocated to death. Without art there would be no more life. For him, spring would never come again.

Chapter 3

Jicky's Thoughts of Spring

What would Jicky's idea of spring be?

Romantic love and poetry? This is not hard to imagine given her romantic and sentimental nature, which could easily be summed up with a famous aphorism by Nietzsche: 'What should we learn from artists... What means have we for making things beautiful, attractive and desirable when they are not so?...We, however, want to be poets of our lives, and first of all in the smallest and most commonplace matters.'[39]

Unearthing the identity of Jicky's love, the mysterious French Resistance fighter, partner and the father of her only child, was hard work. Jicky never spoke of him willingly. Perhaps he had not been her great love as she had thought. Imprisoned by the Germans, he wrote her notes from his cell saying how he could not wait for the baby. Instead, she gave birth alone in a dark little room, lit only by candles and providentially assisted by nuns, as she later recounted. There was no mention of the presence of her man. He might still have been in prison or fighting in the war. But Jicky had erased all traces of him afterwards. This was Jicky's typical attitude when she was hurt by someone, making it more likely that he had later abandoned her.

Jicky never hid her colourful love life. On the contrary, she bragged about it. Yet she never did anything half-heartedly; her passions and romances were all genuine. A nonconformist and an incurable bohemian, it was no problem for her to admit that she was pregnant out of wedlock, although in those years, it was considered a scandal in the puritanical Anglo-Saxon world. A true taboo, a disgrace even in her professional context.

Being the rock of scandal was a badge of honour for her to display. A feather in her cap, a boast. A real provocateur. And if someone talked behind her back? As the French writer and painter Francis Picabia said: 'My ass contemplates those who talk behind my back.' Jicky, being the classy lady she was, would not have pronounced the word 'ass', but in meaning, the attitude was identical. Let us also remember that Jicky had already become pregnant by a previous partner she had met in Brussels, Charles. It did not work out then. She lost the baby she was carrying, whom she would have loved to name Claudia.

According to the studies that Jicky undertook with Professor Madame Ania Teillard, an expert psychoanalyst and graphologist who was Jung's disciple, the psyche governed by laws is a system that is held with oppositions such as instinct and spirit that underlie the tension called psychic energy or libido. Psychic energy is governed by libido. In fact, it is the same thing. One only has to dwell on this basic concept of her studies to understand why the sentimental/sensual life was so fundamental to Jicky. It was her psychic balance, even in the dark years of the war, while she was carrying out the extremely dangerous activity of spying against the Nazis.

Realising that finding her spring spirit in a new love was a given, this gave her the strength to fight and to hope. To forget the death that surrounded her and the fear of being arrested. 'Death and sorrow will be the companions of our journey; hardship our garment; constancy and valour our only shield. We must be united, we must be undaunted, we must be inflexible.' These were Churchill's words to the war-weary population.

Jicky was on the front line in Paris fighting the Nazis and helping the French Resistance. She would have naturally had a French partisan partner. A real Resistance fighter, but who was he? Tracking him down has proved very difficult, primarily because few of Jicky's friends knew of his existence. Dorothy, her great friend, knew that Claude was not the legitimate son of Mr Juvénal, that scion of the Hermès family, the refined gentleman who gave him paternity.

Dorothy was aware that Claude was the son of the Resistance fighter, but she did not know his name. Even her son Claude was in the dark, growing up believing himself to be the true son of Mr Juvénal. When he found out the truth as an adult, it was a real shock for him, and he insistently asked his mother for information.

Yet his real father, the Resistance fighter, could not have disappeared just like that, all traces erased, vanished from the world.

Those who knew Jicky knew that she kept everything tidy in her notes and diaries. At home, she kept a kind of archive, with thematic folders dedicated to each person in her life. There was one on Pascale Mussard, where there were photographs, letters and newspaper articles about her. In her friend Nicoletta's there were postcards from London, Germany and Florence that she had sent her over the years, as well as the invitation to the painting exhibition and the booklet dedicated to Nicoletta's zodiac sign, Cancer.

'Whoever conceives a child with someone,' explains single mother Sabra, an Italian-American friend of Nicoletta's, 'cannot afford to lose all trace of their partner, even if they have behaved badly. A bond will always be there. He is the father of your child.' So, it only took this small glimmer to reopen the investigation into the nebulous Resistance fighter, Jicky's partner in Paris during the war, who was arrested by the Gestapo alongside her and taken to prison.

The search started with Jicky's notes and address book. Only in them could one hope to find some inspiration. It was a frantic search, sometimes even in the middle of the night. The stakes were too high. To uncover yet another undiscovered fact from the Second World War, a piece that might be lost forever swallowed up in oblivion. And again, quoting Winston Churchill, whose proverbial quotes set the standard and forged history: '...It is a riddle, wrapped in a mystery inside an enigma.' In this instance, he was referring to the Soviet Union, but it fits perfectly with the research of this Frenchman of the Resistance, Jicky's companion in those years.

I decided to go through Jicky's notes, diaries and phonebook again, trying to extrapolate some information about the mysterious French fighter. I transcribed all the French names I found, flagging several of them, with four or five being the likely ones. As a second move, I attempted to seek documentary confirmation from the French authorities, although naturally, I carried out the search from Italy.

I discovered, after a long series of unsuccessful attempts by contacting the various French Resistance foundations, that the historical material belonging to the Second World War has not been digitised. Nothing is available on the internet. Every document is strictly paper only. Both classified and declassified. One understands the reasons for not adding the information in such a manner; transferring it to the internet could mean it is intercepted. There is no longer any confidentiality on the internet and any data can be read, especially any classified, i.e. not public, information.

Both the French Resistance foundations and even more so the French Defence Historical Service in Vincennes are firmly anchored to this ironclad rule. Probably by law. Every single document can only be granted by them and never by e-mail, but by hand. The French Defence Historical Service only has a part of its documents on the internet. Mostly lists of names.

My research on the French guerrilla fighter, which had begun years ago, thus suffered a further setback, given that the pandemic had hindered any travel to France. After an initial hard start, I proceeded stubbornly, without further hesitation. Although, in reality, an issue had arisen. How could it be proved that Jicky had transcribed her former partner's name, given that after a period living together in Paris during the war, and after having a child together, he was back behind the scenes, in the shadows? The answer was contained in those little diaries. They betrayed Jicky's way of thinking, that uncommon precision and rationality, as previously mentioned. She had a scientific background, like all the members of Churchill's 'army of intellectuals'.

Eccentric, over the top, but with the attitude of a scientist even in the small everyday things. Churchill himself was outside of the box. An intellectual, of ill health, not a man of vigour. 'When Hitler came to power, Churchill did not use judgement but one of his deep insights... That was what we needed,' wrote C.P. Snow, the scientist and wartime spymaster. Intuition was his trump card, with judgement being of little use given the overwhelming German wartime supremacy over the British.

For every British plane, the Germans had three. And for every British soldier, the Germans had two. The British also had fewer weapons and equipment. To threaten Churchill, Hitler had said, referring to the devastated Warsaw: 'Gentlemen, you have seen for yourselves what criminal folly it was to defend this city,' adding angrily, 'I only hope that certain statesmen in other nations who want to turn the whole of Europe into a second Warsaw, may have the opportunity to see, as you have, the true meaning of war.' No one had been more perceptive than Churchill in understanding what war meant to Hitler, who had declared that the best and most exciting day of his life was the outbreak of the First World War. It made him as excited as a shark who smells blood.

'...When we see the originality of malice, the ingenuity of aggression, which our enemy displays,' Churchill warned, 'we may certainly prepare ourselves for every kind of novel stratagem and every kind of brutal and treacherous manoeuvre...'[40] Hence the choice of this new kind of 'soldier', an advanced formula of fighters. The army of intellectuals, capable of inventing any kind of stratagem and manoeuvre thanks to a flicker of inventiveness and intelligence, to the art of improvising.

In his book *Natural Born Heroes*,[41] the American journalist Christopher McDougall perfectly describes these new characters of Churchill's army of intellectuals. He speaks of them as lonely ghosts with the inventiveness and self-confidence to test 'the unwritten laws of war', as Churchill put it, and execute whatever havoc they dreamed up.

They were lethal shadows ready to haunt the Nazis' sleep, to frighten them. Churchill kept the military to fight in the war, to destabilise.

Biographer William Manchester wrote in *The Last Lion* that Churchill 'was not made of the stuff that makes up a gladiator'. He also wrote that as a young man, Churchill was sickly, with pale girlish hands who was bullied by classmates at school. But Churchill had been able to turn that bullied and mocked youth first into a witty war correspondent and officer, and then into the saviour of Europe's freedom. For these reasons, he would choose men and women like him. He would select archaeologists, poets, professors, linguists and people with travel experience. People with false passports capable of inventing new identities. Adventurers. 'We were amateurs, 100 per cent total amateurs and it couldn't be any other way,' declared Basil Davidson, one of these characters.

The island of Crete, a land unconquered by the Nazis, is the most striking example. Patrick Leigh Fermor, poet and archaeologist, a bohemian and romantic type, was the architect of Nazi nightmares. After a long period on the island mingling with the natives, sent by the British government, Patrick, known to everyone as Paddy, came up with the bizarre idea to kidnap the Nazi officer General Heinrich Kreipe.

And he succeeded. Aided by other Cretans and two or three British agents, the German general disappeared into thin air on 14 April 1944. They did not kill Kreipe but treated him as a prisoner of war. To frighten the other Nazis afterwards, Paddy left a note in the general's car saying that the British raiding force had kidnapped the Nazi officer and transferred him off the island. Then he had left traces of the British matrix of the action in the car: an Agatha Christie book, Cadbury's milk chocolate wrappers, a British army cap and cigarette butts, also of British make. All this to avoid reprisals by the Nazis against the local population. Not to be outdone by a good dose of British humour, Paddy left a P.S. written in the note: 'We are very sorry to have to leave this beautiful motor car behind.' The Nazis, meanwhile, believed it had been the work of a commando unit and not a couple of quirky British agents accompanied by some Cretan peasant.

These men were Jicky's colleagues and she was one of them. A fantasist but still a careful planner. So, it was obvious, Jicky would have written down somewhere in her notes the name of the French fighter. I needed to think the same way she did in order to find him. It was enough to analyse how her colleagues operated to gain confirmation of the mental dynamics they followed. Reason and imagination. Enterprise and culture. Intelligence and great precision. Above all, a flair for great insights.

Chapter 4

Desperately Seeking Gerard Vogel

Help came from France. With the list of French names found in Jicky's address book, I contacted de Gaulle's Free France Foundation without knowing if the man I was looking for was in this group. I also did not know whether Jicky had written down his real name in the address book or his battle name, the one used by many French Resistance fighters so as not to be discovered.

After a phone call with de Gaulle's Free France Foundation in Paris, in which I provided names to check, I received an email from Sylvain Cornil-Frerrot, the Head of Historical Research. Sylvain had checked the historical books on the French Resistance in the Foundation's archives in Paris, and one of the names I had given him, which I had found in Jicky's diaries, was similar to one of the French Resistance fighters proclaimed by de Gaulle from his London exile. Jicky had written Lucienne Durand, who, as I later found out, had been Claude's nanny.

Sylvain well understood the importance of my historical research and the unpublished work I was working on. I told him about Jicky's notes and that, at the time of her arrest by the Gestapo, she had been living with this Frenchman, who was also captured by the Nazis. His email stated:

> I found neither Mr. Krutoff nor Georges Cabon. On the other hand, there is a Lucien Durand, born March 11, 1908 in Lorient (Morbihan). The Historical Defence Service at the Château de Vincennes has a file with his name listed: GR 16 P 203963. We have no more information about him.

Lucien Durand was indeed one of the French Resistance fighters. This similarity of name to Claude's nanny, Lucienne Durand took me a long time to research. On the phone with the Free France Foundation, the pronunciation of Lucienne could have been similar to Lucien. I continued with the search.

After this invaluable help, I had no choice but to turn to the French Defence Historical Service at Vincennes. Although Jicky's Resistance man was not Lucien/Lucienne Durand, I believed they could still help me with my research.

Thanks to Claude's friends, I finally learned that the real name of Jicky's partner was Gerard Vogel. In fact, her son Claude's middle name was Gerard. My search for Gerard in France lasted almost two years. There were fruitful days, alongside others of discouragement. The mistake stemmed from the fact that I had been looking for the wrong name. It was Gerard Vogel, not Lucien Durand. This can often happen in historical research. A lot of time and effort is taken searching for people who, in the end, turn out not to be the ones you are looking for. Mistakes are not allowed when writing about history, so it is better to take your time when researching than to make blunders.

My investigation had started from afar. I had contacted the French Defence Historical Service. After a series of phone calls and finding the e-mail address of the Head of Historical Research, they replied to me, categorically and politely, that they did not send material by e-mail. To gain access to the documentation one had to make an appointment, book a month, a month and a half in advance if possible, and go directly to the Château de Vincennes, near Paris. Alternatively, after booking in advance, I could send someone I trusted with my proxy and a copy of my attached documents.

I was very hopeful. Their historical archive held the identity card of Lucien Durand, a French Resistance fighter during the Second World War. Although he was not Jicky's partner, his story intrigued me. He was an unknown, so I continued to investigate him. A probable comrade-in-arms of Gerard Vogel who unfortunately, like Jicky, had left no archival traces of himself. Another lonely ghost.

I tried again to contact the Historical Service, explaining that it was impossible for me to go to France during the pandemic period. The secretary suggested I send a formal request by registered mail, explaining the reasons for my urgency in receiving Lucien Durand's document and my inability to go to France during lockdown. I sent the registered letter the same day with the hope of having bypassed the problem and the oppressive bureaucracy. Unfortunately, my registered letter was never answered.

After a few months, I tried a new strategy. I contacted the Head of Historical Research again, and finally received a reply from David Sbrava, the Head of Public Information.

He immediately understood that I could not travel to Vincennes, not because I did not respect French laws in this regard, or to ask for favouritism, but because of the international lockdown. I simply could not travel from Rome, the city where I work.

Grateful for the dispensation he granted me, I asked him to allow me to have the document sent to my house. Otherwise, my search would be permanently blocked. He instructed one of his co-workers to contact me and ask for my home address, specifying that he would need a couple of months to send the document. After two months, given the absence of the precious missive, I contacted the invaluable Mr Sbrava again. After my reminder, the letter was sent from Vincennes within a week. After a few days, the envelope with document was finally in my hands, even though in the end, it was not the document I was hoping for for Jicky's Frenchman.

Chapter 5

A French Identity Document with a London Stamp

Although Lucien Durand was not Jicky's partner, after analysing the entire document I realised that this other Resistance man from France was worthy of interest for my research. From him, we are able to see how many of Gerard Vogel's non-famous colleagues in the Resistance lived. Excerpts from their lives. From a trivial misunderstanding came an unprecedented piece of history.

I have a copy of Lucien Durand's French identity papers. The first thing that jumps out is that it was issued in London, although this was normal given that General de Gaulle followed the operations of his Free French Resistance movements from the British capital, whose Free French Forces Headquarters was at 3 Carlton Gardens in St. James'. De Gaulle was aided by General Philippe Leclerc de Hauteclocque, the war hero who was considered the liberators' strong arm, the designated liberator of Paris when Eisenhower gave him the order to liberate the capital on 20 August 1944. Upon learning that de Gaulle was organising the Free French Forces (from 1942 France Combatant) from London, Leclerc immediately joined the fight with courage and resourcefulness, achieving multiple military victories. He died in 1947 in Algeria in a plane crash.

Lucien Durand's papers are interesting, even if he was not our man. His real name was used rather than a nickname invented to protect him from the Nazis. Nevertheless, all the combatants used nicknames. Some groups used the names of Paris metro stations, others those of flowers. Their identity papers said a lot about these valiant guerrilla soldiers, hunted like animals, in hiding and with no real identity. If

Jicky was a spook, a spectre because of her secret list in the British Secret Service, these people were real ghosts with documents issued by another state, Britain.

De Gaulle had not bowed like Pétain to the Nazis. He had fled to Britain. France had summoned him home, but following his refusal, a court martial declared him a deserter of war and a death sentence hung over his head. Britain had been the only nation in Europe unwilling to bow down to Hitler, and so it was that Winston Churchill welcomed de Gaulle to London with open arms.

On 18 June 1940, the day after his arrival in London, de Gaulle made his short but intense speech to the French via BBC radio. Not all French people were able to hear him, but word of mouth had a great impact on people's consciences. It was a famous call to arms.

> ...Must hope disappear? Is defeat final? No!
> ...I, General De Gaulle, currently in London, invite the officers and the French soldiers who are located in British territory ... to put themselves in contact with me.
> ...Whatever happens, the flame of the French resistance must not be extinguished and will not be extinguished.

From his first meeting in London with Churchill, de Gaulle had already earned the support and recognition of the British Prime Minister. At Downing Street on 27 June, Churchill said to him: 'You are all alone. Well then, then I recognise you alone.'

We now know that the relationship between the two was not idyllic. De Gaulle used outdated means of communication with his men, coded messages that were easy to understand and were therefore intercepted and decrypted by the Nazis. When the British warned him, de Gaulle, sceptical, continued to use them, so much so that Churchill – as well as the Americans – no longer passed on important military information. They cut him off, which irritated him enormously.

As General Edward Louis Spears, Churchill's personal representative to the Free French, had declared: 'Of all the crosses I have to bear, the heaviest is the Cross of Lorraine.' Churchill later remarked: 'England's grievous offence in de Gaulle's eyes is that she has helped France. He cannot bear to think that she needed help. He will not relax his vigilance in guarding her honour for a single instant.'

On the other hand, in his moving speech on 25 August 1944 from the Hôtel de Ville, de Gaulle exclaimed:

> Paris! Paris outraged! Paris broken! Paris martyred! But Paris liberated! Liberated by itself, liberated by its people with the help of the French armies, with the support and the help of all France, of the France that fights, of the only France, of the real France, of the eternal France!

Not a single word of thanks to the Allies who had helped, protected and liberated her. No mention of the SOE, the SIS or the Office of Strategic Services (OSS), the American intelligence service who assisted the French resistance.

The Italian politician Umberto Bossi once said that 'gratitude is the virtue of the day before,' but this lack of gratitude to Britain and America greatly offended them. It was a ridiculous and grotesque way of trying to rewrite history. De Gaulle's intention was to restore cohesion to the nation, always clinging to his deep nationalist thinking. He wanted to recompose national unity, dusting off the pride of the French while knowing that he was inventing a non-existent page of Second World War history. He had to rebuild his nation from its ashes and reformulate its political system. He had to make the French forget the sense of cowardice they felt in their hearts at the humiliation of having had to succumb to the German occupiers. That sense of frustration that the professor and man of letters Jean Guéhenno described so well in the aforementioned *Journal des années noires*. France was in ruins, ruled by the black market and smugglers. Reconstruction was a priority.

In neglecting to thank his allies, de Gaulle also increased the importance of his role in the war. The former occupied nations, once liberated, no longer harboured any love for their liberators. It is a practice established over centuries. To start again, they must erase the shame suffered with a burst of pride. As for the saviours, better to forget them.

But let us leave the historical judgements to the historians.

Chapter 6

Resistance Fighters Lucien Durand and Gerard Vogel

Returning to Lucien Durand, even if the trail turned out to be wrong, a very interesting page of history began to emerge. The date on Lucien Durand's identity paper is 3 March 1942, although under the date of incorporation into the Legion, 7 August 1940 is listed. This means that Lucien Durand was among the very first to enlist in the ranks of de Gaulle's Resistance, the Forces France Libre.

One can read the number of the identity paper, Fiche N° 10723, which is written with a stamp. Among the other identity documents produced is the military and family mobilisation booklet written in pen. Next to the entry grade, a blank space. Durand was not a graduate. Neither officer nor non-commissioned officer. Or perhaps this was meant to be secret? His civilian profession is listed as an assembly worker.

He is not listed as having any special skills (a driving licence, for example), nor is he listed as knowing any foreign languages, so one must assume that he only spoke French. His family status is given as single, and his family address, (optional): Madame Nicole, 6 Rue Marie Dorval Lorient (Morbihan). This was actually the address of a business run by Madame Nicole Le Pogam, specialising in the repairs of personal and household goods.

Under 'expressed desires', it is written that Lucien Durand wished to join the merchant navy.

Another entry lists Durand's military specialisation as 'cook'. This entry is rather funny if you imagine a guerrilla fighter who specialises as a cook, but he must have undergone this particular training at some point. Who at that time of war, hunger and cold could have afforded a cook? True, he aspired to join the merchant navy and would have had that specialisation in the ship, but to imagine him cooking delicacies seems rather unlikely. And certainly not cooking nouvelle cuisine. In addition, Resistance fighters were hiding in the bush, in the mountains as already mentioned.

The recruitment office is given as Lorient, Brittany, meaning he was recruited in his hometown. His date and place of birth was 11 March 1908 in Lorient (Morbihan), and his nationality, naturally, was French. Under the other headings such as physical aptitude, etc. the spaces were left blank. In the fingerprint box were imprints of his index fingers and then above, the place: London, but the date is absent. Finally, his signature completes the document. It is a firm signature, well set on the paper. Jicky taught us that if well imprinted, a person's handwriting denotes strength and health. Durand's 'D' is rather flamboyant, almost in contrast to what we might imagine about a tough, virile guerrilla. In the space reserved for a photograph, nothing.

The identity of Lucien Durand was finally revealed.

Another unpublished, very important document I discovered on Lucien Durand is the one found in the historical archives of American hospital admissions during the Second World War. Again, the search was long, but ultimately fruitful. The satisfaction of finding unpublished historical papers repays the hard work of research and the time spent.

In the document, the date of Lucien Durand's hospitalisation in 1944 is listed, as well as his personal data such as his birth in 1908, that he was in the military branch of infantry, and his medical diagnosis, from which we learn that although he was young, only 36, he was already suffering from haemorrhoids. The treatment for haemorrhoids includes a clamp and ligation, so one can guess how much he may have suffered, undergoing such a delicate surgery in a military field hospital.

In those wartime days, many young people fell ill due to the poor diet and terrible living conditions. Hiding in the cold, accompanied by sleepless nights, filled with adrenalin, they fed themselves as best they could, based on what they could find. Many of them fell ill with gastrointestinal disorders, and these were likely the reasons for Durand's illness and subsequent operation at the US army field hospital. As a young, strong man, it is unlikely to have been otherwise since, according to the hospital's medical report, he had not been hospitalised for gunshot wounds. Once discharged, he returned to fight with his Resistance comrades.

In the end, the decision to find out more about Lucien Durand turned out to be very satisfying, even if he was not Jicky's boyfriend. It provided an unprecedented glimpse into a now-forgotten Resistance character.

***

Documents on Gerard Vogel could not be found at the French Defence Historical Service when I asked for them. According to Antony Beevor and Artemis Cooper's book, *Paris After the Liberation 1944-1949*,[42] Resistance fighters came from different backgrounds and there were several Resistance organisations. Many were in charge of rescuing airplane pilots and crews of Allied troops or escaped prisoners of war, while others collected sensitive data for Allied intelligence. Others hid Jews, distributed leaflets and propaganda; the role of saboteurs and those who carried out military actions was crucial.

De Gaulle's supporters were not great in number. The France Libre troops consisted of no more than two battalions from either the survivors of Dunkirk or the expeditionary forces sent to Norway, and were joined by a group of officers and sailors who had escaped from the French metropolitan areas, either individually or in small groups. Remember that in Lucien Durand's papers issued in London, he had aspired to enlist in the merchant navy.

In addition to the volunteers, de Gaulle had hoped to bring together troops from overseas colonial forces. The French Resistance comprised a remarkable mix of political and social forces. Along with the aforementioned regular officers, there were socialists, students both left-wing and Catholic, communists, Spanish republicans and monarchists. De Gaulle's aim was for an apolitical army, which would have been stronger vis-à-vis England and the United States after victory, taking away their ability to impose military rule in France under the pretext of internal dissent. Such a danger could be averted by uniting the resistance groups under his apolitical command.

The British were relieved that the Resistance had developed in three ways: groups supported by British intelligence, groups loyal to de Gaulle (Gaullists) and finally, the communists. Early in the war, it was actually the communists who were most prepared to take direct action against the Germans. As German reprisals included killing ten locals for every German killed, however, many people opposed the communists themselves.

One of the most famous supporters of the French Resistance was the painter Pablo Picasso, who had joined the communist party, arousing criticism in right-wing circles. In reality, he had become the most suitable spokesman for recruiting new forces for the communists. Yet we are sadly still no closer to understanding who Gerard Vogel was. Contacts with London are obvious, demonstrated by his proximity to Jicky, who was an effective British operative. He was also likely a Gaullist. Jicky always claimed to have 'lent a hand' to de Gaulle's Free French Resistance groups, so it is not impossible that Gerard Vogel may have been of that persuasion.

Chapter 7

Lucienne Durand, Josephine Baker and the 18th Arrondissement

The name that had caused the misunderstanding which later proved useful was that of Lucienne Durand. The name was included in Jicky's notebooks, and she was one of her friends, chosen as Claude's nanny.

In the personal column, Jicky had written:

Lucienne Durand
5 Villa Dancourt 18
Orn. 29-93

There was no telephone number.

It is the address where Claude's nanny used to live, in the Montmartre district of Paris. We do not know if Jicky had also lived here with her French companion, Gerard Vogel, when they were caught together by the Gestapo. She had certainly noted this as her address in her diary. Jicky had later reported that she had bought a studio in the centre of Paris.

One discovers with amazement that Josephine Baker, like Lucienne Durand, also lived in Villa Dancourt during the Second World War. She was also involved in de Gaulle's Resistance and joined the French counter-espionage during the war.

But perhaps this is not a mere coincidence. Perhaps many Resistance fighters lived in this Paris neighbourhood, the 18th arrondissement. American-born Josephine Baker was mainly known for her artistic qualities, as a singer, dancer and actress. She had graced the stages of the most prestigious theatres in France, but her greatest quality was undoubtedly courage, which she displayed when she joined the Resistance and the French Secret Service during the war. In 2021, President Macron decided to honour her with a place in the Panthéon, normally reserved for French nationals.

Josephine would certainly have been worthy of Winston Churchill's admiration, who considered courage a person's most important quality because it guarantees all others. When Baker refused to perform in Paris in front of a group of Germans, an unthinkable act at the time, it certainly took a lot of courage.

We do not know if Jicky knew Josephine Baker. They certainly both frequented the 18th arrondissement, and as Claude's nanny, Lucienne, lived in Villa Dancourt, alongside Josephine, it is possible that the two may have met.

Based on the research undertaken on the French Resistance, including the aforementioned book by Anthony Beevor and Artemis Cooper, the 18th arrondissement in Paris was populated by the working class. Many had become communists during the Resistance in the hope that victory would lead to revolution, which was still very relevant among the French. This area of Paris was often the scene of many vicissitudes during the Second World War, the most ferocious actions. On one occasion, a prostitute who had had relations with many Germans was kicked to death by citizens.

In 1947, at the beginning of the post-war economic recovery and the revival of the fashion industry, when Christian Dior organised photograph shoots with models in various areas of Paris, they took place initially in Montmartre, in the 18th arrondissement. Displays of anger erupted in this area among the local people, who were still suffering from the hardships of years of misery. Several women from the neighbourhood beat up one of the models, tearing off her clothes and hair.

Meanwhile, in the central workshops of the French railways, still in the 18th arrondissement, young communists worshipped their older brothers who were considered heroes because they had participated in the Resistance. They met in basketball clubs and on Sundays, people would dress up to go and sell Communist Party newspapers. Young communists were very active here, as were the young Catholics, who met in the local churches.

Singing and dances called *la goguette* were also organised in this neighbourhood, where the young people danced to the notes of swing and bebop. The Communist Party did not want to maintain its anti-jazz diktat so as not to lose the younger members of its ranks, so various sections organised meetings and convivial lunches. May Day, workers' day, was also celebrated. The working class of the neighbourhood had not managed to amalgamate with the intelligentsia, as was the case in other areas, where the intellectuals had managed to assimilate perfectly. Despite this, the young children of the working class were urged to educate and improve themselves.

De Gaulle was convinced that the communists wanted power, and considered the Communist Party as a threat to his authority. However, he was forced to take into account their power gained during the underground struggle. Nevertheless, for Winston Churchill, all Resistance members and partisans were fundamental to the cause; a vital pillar to be united with all others. Consequently, he sent them economic and military aid, which was distributed through the intermediary of British secret agents who were also called upon to help the local populations.

Although Lucienne Durand lived in this specific area of Paris, the heart of the Parisian Resistance, it is not known exactly to which political current she belonged and how she met Jicky. Certainly, Jicky must have trusted her implicitly, otherwise she would not have entrusted her with her child.

Chapter 8

Gerard Vogel in Prison

When I discovered, via Claude's friends in Paris, that Jicky's real partner, Claude's father, was Gerard Vogel, I could not help but notice, as previously discussed, that Claude's middle name was also Gerard, a name clearly given by Jicky in honour of his father. He was Claude Gerard Smith and took Jicky's maiden name until Jean Juvénal, Jicky's husband, legitimised him when Claude was already of a certain age.

Gerard Vogel is not on the official lists of de Gaulle's Free France Foundation. It is not known why. Gerard Vogel could have used a cover name like many others. Or, since he was Jicky's partner, a British intelligence agent, it is possible that his name was never included in the Resistance lists, so as to provide greater protection. Or was it simply because he did not have such a prominent role. It is all supposition. We do not know why his name is not included on the official lists of French fighters. He was another ghost, like Jicky.

It is through Claude's first wife Paola, who had seen a photograph, the only one in Claude's possession, of his father with Jicky, smiling in summer clothes, probably taken before Claude was born, that we discover Gerard Vogel was very similar to Claude himself. In the photograph, Gerard appears taller than Jicky, who was herself tall and light-haired, although his hair is somewhat receding. Vogel is a typical surname in Alsace France, but nothing else is known about his family of origin and where he was born.

Claude had shown Paola some notes written in pencil that Gerard had given to Jicky from the prison where he was imprisoned. Jicky was held in Avenue Foch, so Gerard might have been there too. He wrote that he thought a lot about her and the baby and that he hoped they could soon be reunited. But that did not happen.

Gerard Vogel returned to the theatre of battle, or perhaps he was still in prison, leaving Jicky to give birth alone. It is not known whether they had broken up in the meantime or had drifted apart because of the war. They were certainly no longer together. What is undeniable is that Jicky gave birth on her own in a semi-dark room, lit by the flames of a few candles and helped by nuns. Or at least, this is what she often repeated later in life.

Even in her glory years, at the height of her splendour, Jicky often returned to talk about the past. The darkest pages of her history. Despite her cheerfulness, her carefree and loving nature, her optimism in looking to the future, and her exemplary strength, those ugly refrains within a beautiful song were repeated.

Jicky lived for the future. She did not want to live in the past, but it was the past that lived in her. The problem was that she was left alone with a child and the war still raged on. The French were suffering all kinds of hardships, including cold and hunger, on top of everything else. The winter of 1943/44 had been particularly cold, and Jicky repeatedly told of her freezing prison at the time of her arrest in Paris. Indeed, that winter was so severe that the RAF ordered the Special Duties Squadron to postpone all their flights.[43]

Jicky was helping the French Resistance and at the same time working for the British Secret Service. She had signed the Official Secrets Act, the law for the protection of state secrets that was enacted in 1911 by the British government, which meant imprisonment or even execution for agents who revealed their activities to an outsider. Always respectful of the signed legislation, Jicky knew very well that she could not reveal her activities to anyone. She had demonstrated this with great courage when she was captured and imprisoned by the Gestapo. Not a word had come out of her mouth. Even under torture. The Secret Intelligence Service (SIS) was famous for its strict silence. Always and forever. Remember that Jicky's gravestone in Sirolo gives her name as Jicky, not Hazel, her real name. Her surname, meanwhile, is given as Juvénal, that of her French husband, and not her maiden name of Smith.

Crucially, Jicky received a salary for her survival and that of her new-born child. It is not known how she received the money and from whom, but the secret services, in order not to leave traces, used to pay in cash. In his book *Churchill's School For Saboteurs*, Bernard O' Connor writes that, at the end of the war, the British intelligence officer Commander Arthur Langley, admitted that the rules of engagement for secret agents were rather simple:

> One was not officially employed by anyone. One was paid in cash; there was no security, no pension or health plan. One did not render any income tax return. Officially one had failed to exist. An assignment would be given to fulfil as best one could, usually outside the law; if one was caught either by the police of one's own country or the counter-intelligence organisation of another, one would be officially disowned.[44]

This confirms that Jicky, once left alone, was able to completely provide for her basic needs. She must also have been helped by her network of people in the French Resistance, as well as a network of British people who were cooperating in France with de Gaulle's Free France groups.

Chapter 9

The Mystery of Jicky's British Colleagues in the French Resistance

Thanks to the research undertaken in the French archives at Vincennes, under the aegis and management of the person in charge, David Sbrava, my historical insights had developed considerably. Mr Sbrava had been instrumental in acquiring relevant documents on the resistance, but now it was time to investigate whether Jicky had left traces of her existence in France in the same archives; a difficult task given her excellent ability to change her name and surname and suddenly disappear in a shroud of mystery.

I asked David Sbrava if he could look in the archives for a Hazel Smith, known as Jicky. He informed me that he had found similar names of other English women, but with different dates of birth. With his help, I came into the possession of codes to other files on British women who had cooperated with the French Resistance. Unfortunately, we have no tangible evidence of their involvement with the British government. Nor of a direct acquaintance with Jicky, although it is assumed that, working in the same Resistance network in France, they could have worked with each other. Jicky could have been the contact person liaising with the British government, with the other women having different roles.

One of the women was Margareth Hazel Venables, who was classified as a volunteer and was likely one of a number of English people who had moved to France voluntarily to do their service. Margareth was born on 14 July 1928 in Kent. As a profession she had indicated that she was a saleswoman. She lived in Ilford, Essex and in her family status was listed as unmarried. It is striking that the document specifies she was a Catholic, as it is hard to imagine a young, single, Catholic shop assistant from England alone in Nazi-occupied France. She certainly could not have survived by herself.

That is until one examines the same document and sees the name of her father. She was the daughter of Edward Venables, an Englishman in his early fifties, who served in British naval intelligence. Later in the war, he was imprisoned by the Japanese in Hong Kong.

This British girl was certainly well connected in France and was perhaps not as alone as previously thought, certainly thanks to her father's connections. The volunteer ring in France was also run by the British Secret Service, as one would have expected. According to the document, Margareth had two brothers and a sister, who were about 23/25 years old. One of her brothers had been taken prisoner at Dunkirk.

The interesting part of this document is the sentence: 'If the volunteer adopts a pseudonym in England, please indicate this at the beginning of this form.' This shows that it was therefore customary to give oneself a false name. However, this was to be specified in the identity document now in the possession of the French Historical Archives.

Margareth Hazel Venables stated that she had already worked in London and Manchester, as well as in Ilford. She had written the word Assurance. Did this mean she had worked in the insurance business? The French government had asked her to provide a British identity document and so she had offered her National Registration Card.

In addition to this, a request appears for the interested party to provide information on the enemy services in question (S.R. (Service de Renseignements), Information Service of the Axis, Gestapo, names of collaborators, etc.). Essentially, this young girl, a volunteer, was asked to carry out actual espionage activities, even though she was not officially enrolled in the intelligence service, neither with the SIS nor the SOE. At least according to this French document.

She was not like Jicky, who, while also being young, was not quite as young as Margareth. She simply worked with the British Resistance. Jicky, on the other hand, was a fully-fledged, enlisted agent. After all, among the other notes made by the examiners on Margareth's document was she did not speak a single word of French. According to her file, she had to collaborate without knowing a single word of the language where she lived, moreover, in a nation occupied by the Nazis. Not like Jicky, who, having moved to Brussels aged about 15, spoke impeccable French.

Margareth was a young English girl who was sent to work more or less as a rookie in France. There is another detail, however, that reminds one a little of Jicky: Jicky's real name was Hazel and her mother Margareth, while this girl was called Margareth Hazel. While these were perhaps common names at the time, it is a strange coincidence.

Let us now turn to the next document found in the French Defence Historical Archives: a certificate issued by the Free French Forces in London on 6 February 1943, approved by proxy. The document is an act of engagement made by Colonel Billot, on behalf of General de Gaulle, to employ a British woman called Marie Robuste for the duration of the war. Once again, we have a young Englishwoman sacrificing her best years for the cause of freedom and democracy. To help a country that was not her own get rid of the Nazi enemy.

Another certificate issued by the Free French Forces to recruit a young British woman can be found in the archives. Her name was Katherine Nancy Hazel. Once more, there is a connection with Jicky's real name, Hazel. Katherine was born on 18 November 1916, making her three years younger than Jicky, who was born on 7 November 1913. A British national, she was born in Beaconsfield, Buckinghamshire.

Like Jicky, Katherine was a graduate and had a French bachelor's degree in literature, as well as a First Class Honours Degree in French from the University of Reading. Besides speaking English (her mother tongue) and French, she also had a good knowledge of German.

Among her former professions, Katherine Hazel wrote that from November to December 1939 she had worked as a secretary at the King Edward VI School in Stafford, and from 1 May 1940 to 1 April 1942, she had worked as a French teacher at Malsis School in Keighley, North Yorkshire.

The documentation is dated 11 February 1942 and was approved with a red stamp on 24 February 1942, with the file number being listed as 41.881. On the back of the sheet is a note from the chief of staff to Commander Passy, head of the BCRAM (*Bureau central de renseignements et d'action militaire*): 'Enclosed is a copy of the information sheet concerning Miss Hazel,' it reads, 'and in view of her qualifications, I thought you might be interested in her candidature. Please let me know your decision on this matter.'

Commander Passy was actually André Dewavrin, who was the head of the Gaullist Secret Service of Free France in London and then Algiers. After hearing de Gaulle's appeal, he immediately joined the Free French Forces in London and created the intelligence service. He undertook very difficult missions when de Gaulle sent him to the occupied zone to spread his directives, gather information and make contacts. Colonel Passy proved to be solid, often lucid and gifted with a sense of organisation. He struggled between intrigues and quarrels.

In 1943 Passy was made a Companion of the Liberation, as a BCRA (*Bureau central de renseignements et d'action*) lieutenant colonel. He had then left London for Algiers with de Gaulle. During the summer, before it was absorbed, strengthened and confirmed by the creation of the DGSS (Special Services Directotate), the BCRA tried to plan the implementation of new military structures in France, attracting, according to Passy, 'the innumerable and tenacious wraths and resentments' of its opponents, who accused it of wanting to slow down the Resistance's transition to armed action. This work led to the formation of groups integrated into the *Forces Francaises de l'Interieur* (FFI), commanded by General Koenig. Parachuted on 5 August 1944 into the Guingamp region to assist the Breton Resistance, Colonel

Passy, at the head of 2,500 FFIs associated with American elements, contributed to the liberation of Paimpol, where 2,000 prisoners were taken.

Katherine Hazel also answered a questionnaire at the time of her recruitment, writing on the form that she could type and write shorthand in both English and French. She was a courageous girl, claiming that she would be willing to go to the colonies, and also demanded '...at least £4 per week' for the job in question, which was supposedly dangerous and consequently required a higher fee.

These women all worked for same network. That of the British Secret Service. They all had similar backgrounds: British, with a strong school and university education. Apart from Margareth, they all had the same knowledge of foreign languages, fundamental to their service in France. Most importantly, they were all ready to make any sacrifice for the cause of democracy and freedom. They were educated young women who set aside their dreams to serve their country and the cause of Europe as a whole.

It is hard to imagine that Jicky/Hazel Juvénal-Smith had not known either Margareth, Katherine or Marie. Or perhaps she was hiding somewhere among the papers themselves?

Chapter 10

The Disappearance and Discovery of Gerard Vogel

We know that Gerard Vogel disappeared completely from Jicky's life, and that he never acknowledged his son. Like many other French Resistance fighters of the Free France group, if Vogel was a communist then he certainly might have had problems with de Gaulle, as their merits were not recognised by the French president after the war. Although de Gaulle had gone to Moscow to sign a pact with Stalin, and Pétain's collaborators had accused him of colluding with the Soviet Union, a year later, de Gaulle immediately took an openly anti-communist stance.

If Vogel had been a Gaullist, however, perhaps he had decided to move abroad and make a new life for himself, rather than try to find a better job in a post-war France that was under reconstruction. Many civilians left war-starved Europe to find their fortunes on other continents, especially North and South America. What is certain is that he disappeared from Europe, although this news would not be confirmed for several years.

Jicky no longer talked about him. As previously discussed, this was typical behaviour by Jicky when she had been hurt by someone. It was as if she had locked him in a drawer and thrown away the key forever. She also removed any personal items, photographs, gifts, letters and cards that might remind her of him. As if she had incorporated some kind of modern computer spam in her head. She would never change her mind again.

Jicky's son Claude, who had remained in Paris when she moved to Italy, discovered the devastating news as an adult, perhaps when he was already working as an established journalist with the French news agency AFP. An authoritative correspondent operating in the most dangerous places in the world, he had become famous over the years. Yet this adult man had to come to terms with the harsh reality. The identity of his real father.

Jicky finally revealed to him that the refined Monsieur Juvénal, with his noble manner, was not his biological father. Juvénal had recognised him, raised him and loved him as if he was his own son, but he was not. Now, for the first time, Jicky told Claude about the valiant fighter of de Gaulle's Free French Forces, and his heroic role in the defeat of Nazism: Gerard Vogel. Once he had recovered from the shock, Claude began to investigate who this man was.

Why Jicky did not reveal the truth to him as a child was obvious: to protect him. A child, knowing that the man he regarded as a father was not his real one, could have grown up with a thousand insecurities and a thousand problems. Instead, she had chosen a truly impeccable father, a gentleman of the French aristocracy.

Jicky revealed to Claude that his father had moved far away from Europe. To South America. To Caracas, Venezuela, to be exact. Like many Europeans, he had emigrated to South America after the war for purely professional and economic reasons. He had rebuilt his life and had established a farm.

I wanted to find out more about Vogel's trip to South America and so examined the journeys made by other Europeans who emigrated to America at that time.

According to the database of arrivals in America, there are no records of a Gerard Vogel from France. Instead, I decided to sift through documents in the Venezuelan embassy in Rome. Unfortunately, the officials could not provide me with documentation of Vogel's transfer to their country. Not even details about his farm. It is likely that he travelled under an assumed name.

I later found out that many fighters from de Gaulle's Free France group had moved to South American states, including Argentina, Venezuela, Uruguay. Indeed, in Uruguay there was even a group called the Free France Committee.

When the Nazis entered Paris on 14 June 1940, the students of Montevideo expressed their grief in a particularly moving demonstration. As soon as General de Gaulle's appeal was launched a few days later, a vast movement of opinion developed that led, on 15 August 1940, to the creation of the 'Franco-Uruguayan Committee for Free France' under the presidency of Dr Maxime Halty, who had been born in Uruguay of a French father and Uruguayan mother.

The equivalent of $42,500 was sent to London from 1940 to 1944 by the Committee, while special collections raised important funds to help prisoners of war and to buy woollen blankets for hospitals in France after the Liberation. Like most overseas committees, the Montevideo committee covered the costs of propaganda, the start-up of its volunteers, the payment of allowances to their families, the shipment of clothes and shoes to refugees, and even the cost of a French radio course: in all, this represented a financial effort of more than $120,000.

Gerard Vogel had moved permanently to Caracas, so Claude decided to fly to Venezuela to meet his real father for the first time. To see his face and hear his voice. Sadly, the result was not what he had hoped it would be. The meeting went badly. Glacial. There was no chance for a recovery of the father-son relationship. His father was very cold and aloof. Firm in his rejection and disavowal. Claude returned to France disconsolate, shocked despite his mature age, and with a great anger inside.

My search for any historical document on Gerard Vogel was almost over. All hope wrecked forever after years of investigation. I had even contacted the former Italian ambassador to Paris, Giandomenico Magliano, who very diligently made the cultural facilities and social affairs service of the embassy available to me. Yet I had not been able to find Gerard Vogel anywhere. I had even looked for him on the site of the Vatican's Secret Archives on prisoners of war. I had also searched for him in the Italian Army Archives in Rome, an inexhaustible source of documentation, but unfortunately without success.

Websites such as Ancestry.com were also particularly unenlightening. I did manage to find a Gerard Vogel, but the name was among the list of prisoners of war from labour camps on the island of Java in Indonesia.

How could my Gerard Vogel, a Frenchman captured by the Nazis in Paris, have got there?

Finally, I decided to visit The National Archives in Kew, London. I had already rummaged through their online portal looking for Gerard Vogel, but had found nothing. I visited the Archives on 31 August 2024 and at this very time an exhibition on prisoners of war was being held. As soon as I arrived, I could not help but read a sign in the entrance hall explaining that 2,300 Italian prisoners of war had been held in labour camps in this same area of London where The National Archives buildings now stand.

The complex of buildings was known as Camp 144 and in July 1945, over 2,000 Italian prisoners of war were being held there. Italy had surrendered in 1943 and many Italian prisoners of war were then categorised as 'co-operators' and put to work outside their camps and granted some freedoms. When not working they could travel for up to 8 kilometres, but were not allowed to visit shops, cinemas or pubs. If invited, they could visit local people in their homes. The 'co-operators' living at Camp 144 worked on properties across London that had been damaged by V1 and V2 rockets. Although the war in Europe ended in May 1945, many Italian prisoners did not start being repatriated until December, as they were still needed for the work they were doing across the country. The final inmates from Camp 144 left Kew in July 1946.

After this discovery, I continued with my research at The National Archives. While I was waiting for some of the searched documents to be examined, I noticed that I was able to access other online ancestry sites that are otherwise unavailable for personal accounts. I typed in Gerard Vogel's name and there he was. At least I assumed it was him. The name Gerard had been Germanised into Gerhardt, predictably, he was a prisoner of the Germans. As already discussed previously, the surname Vogel has Alsatian origins.

I am fairly certain he was there, even if the file contained neither the date, nor the place of birth that would corroborate the truth definitely. It was a miracle.

His name was on a list entitled, 'Imperial Prisoners of War Held in Italy, Italian-Occupied Territory: British & Commonwealth Army'. His qualification was that of lieutenant, his prisoner of war camp was number 47 and he belonged to Regiment number 78897.

My conviction was strengthened when I obtained information, through Italian military channels. I contacted Colonel Emilio Tirone, head of the Italian Army Archives in Rome, asking him for information on where the Italian-occupied territories could have been. I was told they were in the south of France and Corsica. Gerard Vogel was to be imprisoned in those very territories.

At The National Archives I had continued to read everything I could about the prisoners of war. It was reported that more than 75,000 of the prisoners of war held by fascist Italy were recorded by the 'Casualty (PW) Branch of the Directorate of Prisoners of War' in London. The Italian prisoner of war camps' nominal rolls were sourced directly from The National Archives in Kew under the reference WO392/21 and entitled 'Imperial Prisoners of War in Italy'. It was also explained that the main camps were all designated 'PG' (*prigionieri di Guerra*), although they were also abbreviated 'CC' (*Campo di concentramento*). All were prefixed and numbered, with the exception of the two Dulags and one Stalag within Italy, which were German-controlled transit centres for prisoners being transferred to Germany.

When the Italian armistice was announced on 8 September 1943 there were an estimated 80,000 Allied prisoners in Italy. At this point all Senior British Officers (SBOs) informed their men of Field Marshal Montgomery's so-called 'standfast' order, which instructed them to remain in camp and await imminent liberation by the advancing Allied forces.

In the same document in Kew, it was reported that:

Overall victory in Italy took far longer than anticipated. Reaction to the armistice varied from camp to camp. In some, the Italian Commandant refused to hand over control to the

SBO or his equivalent; others opened the gates and disappeared along with the guards. In the latter circumstances, the more perceptive SBOs, realising the Germans would quickly take control, encouraged individual escapes; while some of the more enterprising prisoners escaped without official sanction. Some escapees fled northwards towards Switzerland or southwards towards allied lines. Others hid near their camp to await developments or took the opportunity to explore the vicinity before voluntarily returning to their camp. Ultimately, the confused situation meant that by the end of 1943 some 50,000 POWs had been rounded-up and transported to camps in Germany.

It is not clear whether Gerard (Gerhardt) Vogel managed to escape or was freed, but his name can also be found in a list of medals issued to merchant seamen in the Second World War. It is hard not to notice a similarity here with Lucien Durand, the Resistance fighter who wanted to serve in the merchant navy. Remember, too, that among the ranks of de Gaulle's Free France fighters was a group of officers and sailors who had escaped from France. Vogel, Jicky's boyfriend, who was arrested alongside her in Paris, was later decorated with a medal for valour. Jicky had always said he was a fearless fighter in the face of all dangers. A case of homonymy? Two Gerard Vogels, fighters in de Gaulle's French Resistance who were approximately the same age, prisoners in the same territories and men of great courage. Characteristics that matched perfectly.

PART THREE

Going Home: Jicky's Family, Town and Her Final Secrets

Chapter 1

Jicky's Hometown

Harpenden. Never a word about her pleasant hometown. Never a hint, a reference, a memory. That is, until a James Joyce-like epiphany, a sudden connection triggered between two seemingly distant things, by a simple everyday action. A familiar recurrence. The vision of an event that brought her hometown back into her mind. In her very long life, Jicky never mentioned her beautiful Harpenden. Nothing about the green county of Hertfordshire, in the borough of St Albans. For Jicky, Harpenden, with its nearly 30,000 inhabitants, was like a secret hometown. Only she knew it.

When she recalled memories of her childhood, Jicky was very careful not to reveal that those moments took place in Harpenden. If she described any details about her father, no mention was made of his name. The same for her mother. Jicky told how she had been given a small Bible that also belonged to her mother, but revealed nothing about her life. She said nothing at all about her sisters, of which she had two. Jicky never talked about her family. It was as if they had been characters immersed in a thick fog. In that faint luminous 'mist' that pervades space formed by all the stars in the universe that have existed from the beginning of time to the present.

There was no mention of her move to London. Neither when nor even where. Nor the motivation behind it. Not even why she had been sent to Brussels, when she was about 15 years old, to live with her godparents. Was it only to study?

From Brussels, Jicky then went to Paris, where she worked in the British embassy. On one of her journeys between Brussels and Paris, Jicky was with her Jewish boyfriend at the time, Charles Lieber, whose mother was captured by the Nazis and deported to Auschwitz in 1942. It was probably in Brussels that Jicky was recruited by the British Secret Service. Again, all this was completely confidential. All information about Jicky's birth family came to light later, when she had already passed away. With her documents revealing where she came from, I contacted Harpenden Town Council.

In the first draft of her biography, I had found that Jicky was a native of Harpenden. It had been on her identity document issued by the Italian Ministry of the Interior. There was no mention of her family or residential background, but with the discovery of her true activity as a British secret agent with the SIS, we can understand why.

At the time of their recruitment, active agents were ordered never to reveal anything about themselves, their family members or their hometown. At the outbreak of the Second World War, there was widespread opinion of the great risk of imminent German occupation of Britain, so the withholding of personal information would have safeguarded family members of the secret agents. It was a way of protecting them from the Nazi fury.

Jicky had been born Hazel, but nobody knew this. To everyone she was Jicky. Her surname was Smith, even though her tombstone and her personal documents give it as Juvénal, her French husband's surname. It all fits perfectly with the diktats and rules of British intelligence.

After her death, I gathered all the information about her family history by contacting the Harpenden authorities directly from Italy, using her papers to help me to write the new edition of *L'Angelo Di Churchill*.

Chapter 2

The Discovery of Jicky's Family

After writing Jicky's biography, I decided to delve into her roots via the Harpenden archives. I sent an email and was promptly answered by David Keen with another demoralising response. After all, it was 2020 and the world was still very much in the grip of COVID 19. He replied that he had tried to find evidence of a family named Smith living in a large house in Harpenden, but without success. Smith is a very common name in England, but the records which were accessible at the time did not show a Smith family living in a large house in the area. He suggested that more information might emerge after the COVID crisis was over, but nevertheless, his reply was discouraging.

After this, the archives promptly put me in touch with their history department, whose manager is Mrs Diana Parrott. I informed her that the person I was looking for was called Hazel Smith and that she was born in Harpenden on 7 November 1913. Mrs Parrott kindly let me know that she would undertake the search. Her reply on 22 April reopened the door to hope.

Dear Nicoletta

I can only apologise for the delay in acknowledging your interesting and intriguing email. I hope in the meantime you have stayed free of COVID 19 and are coping with these strange times.

I am not sure we will have to tell you of Hazel Smith's early life in Harpenden. I have checked the index of our archives and nothing shows up for Hazel Smith but that does not mean we have nothing about the family.

Because of lockdown we cannot access our History Room and the library and church are closed, which is where there are such things as street directories, film (microfiches) of a local paper, electoral registers and parish magazines where we might track down such things as where the family lived in Harpenden, how long they were here etc. Even then we really need to know her father and mother's name. I do have access to Ancestry.com at home and have found the birth of a Hazel U. Smith in the correct quarter of the year for her date of birth that you have given me. It was registered at St Albans and that is where a Harpenden birth would have been registered so that fits. Do you know if your Hazel Smith had a middle name starting with a U? The record included the maiden name of her mother – Ashendon [misspelled in original email from Ashenden] and from Ancestry.com a Margaret Emily Ashendon married a Sydney Herbert Smith in Hastings in 1900. Hopefully this is the correct family, but it needs verification and hopefully we might be able to do that but not until places are open again and we are allowed out.

Because it is such an intriguing story we wondered if you would allow us to add your email to our website and perhaps something of it on facebook 'Harpenden in Days gone by' – you never know someones grandmother might have heard something of the story or the family.

Until have more information (hopefully).

Best wishes
Diana Parrott

I was hopeful that this was the family I was looking for. On 7 May, I received another email.

> Dear Nicoletta
>
> I believe things are easing off in Italy, which is good news. We are very much looking forward to the day when we are allowed a bit more freedom.
>
> To Hazel – that extra bit of information could be useful and one of our members has kindly sent for the birth certificate of the Hazel U. Smith, whose birth registration we found on Ancestry, so keep your fingers crossed that it is the correct Hazel. It will take some time to come through so don't expect a quick answer.
>
> Best wishes
> Diana

Two months later, on 18 July, I received a new email with all the documentation on Jicky that the society had eventually managed to find, albeit with difficulty.

> Dear Nicoletta,
>
> I attach what we have found; I hope you can understand it and please do come back to me if you have any questions.
>
> It has taken some time to gather the information; the birth certificate that one of our members kindly ordered took a long time to arrive and we have only just been allowed to access our history room. This was on a specific day and at a specific time; only one couple and to deposit and collect items only – no staying

there to do any research. I requested and received electoral registers which we have and which were a great help.

The birth certificate confirmed Jicky's birth details; told us where the family lived (Kirkwick Lodge and she was apparently born at home) and who the parents were. The electoral registers then told us when they came to Harpenden and how long they stayed. Unfortunately, I don't think there is any way of knowing the family movements after 1928.

Ancestry.com then became our source of information, starting with the England and Wales registration that was taken in 1939.[45]

You will note Sydney remarried after his wife's death, a lady of Italian extraction. It would be interesting to know if there was a connection there but.....!

I think this supports Jicky's memories of Harpenden, although they may have been embroidered – she was only 15 when they left after all. The house is not of Downton Abbey size or grandeur, but it was not a two-up-two-down cottage with no running water either. (I've attached a photo of what is now called Kirkwick Lodge and is probably the Smith's house – it would have been something like it anyway). It had 8 or 9 rooms and it would seem they had a live-in maid like many houses of that size at the time. From the advertisement for a cook (attached) one assumes they had a cook but that reads as though she probably went in daily and the 'knife, boot and coal' boy may well have gone in in the morning before school to do his jobs, but one of those jobs could have been cleaning the silver (it was a 'dirty' job after all). As to horses, there was a field near the house but that doesn't prove anything. However, I imagine Harpenden was a 'horsey' place so there were livery horses/friends' horses that would probably have been available to ride or of course they may have owned a horse/s and kept them in livery. I have attached the 'proof' we have found of the above. Do you have any similar documents of her life during and after the war which you would be willing to share with us?

Hope that is of some interest to you.

Best wishes
Diana

According to her birth certificate, Jicky's real name was Hazel Ursula, but there is also a major error contained in the document. Jicky was born on 7 November 1913, but the certificate gives her date of birth as 17 November. The reason why the Harpenden authorities could not initially find her birth certificate had now been revealed: her birth had likely been registered ten days later, in St Albans.

From her birth certificate, we learn that Jicky was born in Kirkwick Lodge, Kirkwick Avenue, Harpenden. Her father, a shipping merchant, was Sydney Herbert Smith, and had been born in 1872 in Hastings. Her mother, Margaret Emily Smith (née Ashenden) was also born in in Hastings in 1872.

Jicky's mother died in 1944, certainly of illness, in Pinner, north London. Her father was not a widower for long, however, and almost immediately remarried a woman of Italian origin about fifteen years his junior. His new wife, according to the documents, was the professional soprano, Bersabea Francesca.

As discussed previously, Jicky was sent to live with her godparents in Brussels when she was about 15, and it is about the same time that her father sold the house in Harpenden. Throughout her life, Jicky never mentioned her stepmother's name or willingly spoke of her two sisters. Likewise, there were few references to her father. Without ever mentioning his first name or surname, she only said, and even then very rarely, that he was an important textile entrepreneur who made adventurous trips by ship to the East, to countries such as India, to buy precious silks and fabrics for his business. Only once did Jicky mention that in her childhood, she was driven to school in a carriage, and that she had servants at home. She did say that she had an aunt who lived to be 105, but she only said this to boast about her family's longevity. She did mention, however, that her father had allowed British soldiers ready to fight in France during the First World War to camp in the park adjacent to the family home in Harpenden. Jicky befriended one of the soldiers, who in turn gave her a small diary, a medal and a rag doll. Although just a little girl at the time, she would carry those objects with her forever, in memory of that soldier, all the way to Sirolo.

Almost 5,000 soldiers were taken in by local families in Harpenden as they underwent training before leaving for France during the First World War. Henry Tylston Hodgson was one of those who gave asylum to the soldiers. In 1915 and later from 1917-19, his residence was used as a hospital for wounded soldiers. In 2018 the Harpenden & District Local History Society organised an exhibition dedicated to Harpenden and the First World War, which explored what life was like in the town during that time, when school children had to collect eggs and knit socks, and the cinema was busy broadcasting events through Pathé News.

The Harpenden & District Local History Society was an invaluable resource for my research on Jicky and her family. When I presented my book in August 2020 in Sirolo, the town where Jicky resided and is buried, they immediately went into action to accommodate one of my requests: an official greeting in a video from the then mayor of Harpenden, Mrs Nicola Linacre. Her speech was broadcast to the jubilant audience on a giant screen positioned in the centre of Sirolo's square:

> Hello, I am Nicola Linacre, the Mayor of Harpenden and I am very happy to be part of this event today celebrating the life of Hazel Smith, better known to you as Jicky. Jicky was born here

in Harpenden before moving to Sirolo. So, on behalf of everyone in Harpenden, I would like to send my greetings and best wishes to everyone there in Sirolo. Thank you.

As a result of this close cooperation with Harpenden Town Council, I decided to pay a visit to the town at the end of August to learn more about the history of Jicky, her family and her town. I used the opportunity to deliver Jicky's death certificate, which I had meanwhile retrieved from the Sirolo municipality to the historical office in Harpenden. Mrs Rosemary Ross drove me around to let me breathe in the essence of this pleasant town, which lies half an hour by train from London. Mrs Ross and Diana Parrot took me to see the beautiful mansion where Jicky was born. We tried to ring the doorbell of the new owners, unfortunately without success. Nobody was home.

Chapter 3

Secret, Fairytale Harpenden

I arrived in Harpenden almost by chance. As the author of the biography *L'Angelo di Churchill* about the life of Jicky, Hazel Juvénal-Smith, who was born right there in Harpenden on 7 November 1913 and died in Sirolo on 22 January 2011, I was invited by the Local History Society of Harpenden, the municipal body that deals with local history and culture to which the mayor of the town belongs. They learnt of my stay in London in August 2020 and extended the invitation to me. They wanted to show me the villa and the neighbourhood where Jicky was born.

Harpenden is a town in Hertfordshire of 30,000 inhabitants, completely surrounded by greenery. It is about 50 kilometres from London and, I later learned, has become the residential destination of many Londoners who, tired of metropolitan stress, buy a house in this pleasant location and commute to their London offices. Harpenden is also famous for Rothamsted Manor and Rothamsted Research, the experimental agricultural research station, founded in 1843, which has a tradition dating back to 1620 and is under the patronage of the King.

The spectacle on arrival was thrilling. It was 26 August, but the English weather was relentless. Drizzle interspersed with faint rays of sunshine. This in no way obscured the beauty that one saw from the first impact. Diana Parrott, chair of the local history department, and Rosemary Ross, documentary archivist and researcher, took me on a tour of the town.

It is not a town like any other. Green is the dominant feature here. It is present everywhere. An immense scrub dotted with buildings of perfect geometry and antique style. Even in the square in the old town, next to St Nicholas' Church built 800 years ago, near the station and next to the various shops. It is like being in a fairytale town straight out of a book by Hans Christian Andersen or the Brothers Grimm.

Birds can be heard even in the centre and squirrels hop around undisturbed next to the restaurant. There were few people around at that hour, it was almost 11.30 am, and what stood out was that everything was extremely clean. No litter or cigarette butts on the street. No overflowing rubbish bins. Just extremely well-kept villas, ancient trees, bushes and flowerbeds that looked like paintings because of how perfect they were, and these huge expanses of green velvet with blue hues that you were almost afraid of stepping on.

My visit to Jicky's villa was exciting. The current residents, who have lived there for twenty-five years, were unaware of the original owner. Just a few days before, they had learnt that the house had been designed by a famous architect of the time, Percival Blow. A new book about the illustrious architect, *St. Albans Architect: Percival Blow*, had recently been published and included a picture of their own residence inside. Jicky's father, who was very wealthy, had chosen the best architect in England to build their family home.

After multiple photographs and a lunch, we continued with the tour. It was there that I discovered some strange coincidences. Although Harpenden is a small town, I discovered that a man called Esterhazy lived, under a pseudonym, in one of the magnificent cottages, but who was he?

Count Ferdinand Esterhazy was a major in the French army who played a leading role in the biggest judicial and political scandal in late nineteenth-century France, the Dreyfus Affair. The Hungarian-born Count Esterhazy was a French army officer who tried to sell the German military attaché in Paris confidential information about the French army in exchange for money. Despite his noble ancestry, he had a vice for gambling and women and was always short of money. For the deal he obtained 400 francs.

Then, once the high ranks of the French Defence General Staff became aware of information leak and that there was a spy in the military, the blame was placed on Captain Alfred Dreyfus, who came from a Jewish family and was completely uninvolved in the events. Anti-Semitism was rife in French society and so Captain Dreyfus was convicted of espionage and high treason. The seven officers who accused him supported the charges by using false evidence attributed to handwriting experts at the police prefecture. Dishonoured and stripped of his uniform, Dreyfus was condemned without any real evidence and deported to Devil's Island prison, where he could neither speak to anyone, nor write, nor even see the outside world.

Thanks to the obstinacy of his family, as well as the overwhelming evidence of another officer, Colonel Picquart, and writers such as Émile Zola, after many years Dreyfus was freed and he returned to France. However, the real spy all along had been Esterhazy, who was wrongly acquitted and never paid for his misdeeds. After the scandal, he moved to London for a while and then to Harpenden in 1909. Later, again in exchange for money, he revealed to an English newspaper that he had been the real spy in the Dreyfus Affair. He lived in Harpenden with his wife under a false name until his death. They used many pseudonyms over the years, including that of the Counts de Voilement.

I visited his splendid villa in the midst of the greenery, elegant and mysterious. I was told he worked as a journalist for important newspapers, but I wondered how he could have afforded this beautiful mansion given his constant need for money. Someone then revealed that he had become a double agent for the Allies and that he had spied on Germany during a visit.

'He lived simply,' people said. 'At night the neighbours could hear the incessant ticking of the typewriter keys.' 'He used to invite friends from London to dinner at weekends,' said one of his acquaintances, who sometimes attended. 'He was very kind and interesting in the things he told them.'

He had a well-stocked library, with titles on military themes, either of international nature or other literature. Some of the residents remembered him riding his horse around the town, although he also stayed at home and in the garden a lot. His wife went shopping instead. The windows of his house were always locked, especially those in his bedroom. Doors and gates were barred. Trees and bushes planted ad hoc to hide any view.

It was only discovered who he really was after his death. The funeral was held in Our Lady of Lourdes Church in Harpenden. On his grave, the verses of the English poet P.B. Shelley's 'Adonais', v.40: 'He has outsoared the shadow of our night,' raised several objections.

His story brought me back to Jicky: in the Dreyfus Affair, handwriting experts had played a key role. Jicky, meanwhile, was a highly skilled handwriting expert for British intelligence. It was a curious coincidence.

As already discussed, handwriting experts were instrumental in the Dreyfus Affair, leading to Dreyfus' release from prison after years in captivity. Esterhazy's handwriting, the experts claimed, was identical to that of the incriminating sheets of paper.

Esterhazy was never indicted and, by a quirk of history, went into hiding in Jicky's hometown.

I was next taken to visit Rothamsted Manor, which I discovered had been a research centre for agriculture, but during the Second World War the building was used as a military espionage centre. Here, coded messages, encrypted by the Enigma machine, were intercepted from the Nazis and then transmitted to the famous Bletchley Park facility, where they were decoded.

A small town concealed by a magical atmosphere and yet so many cases of espionage? So many spies? Were these simple coincidences or was there more to it? Are there more mysteries that will never be discovered?

Curious, I tried to ask the staff of the history centre a few questions. They were all very knowledgeable; for them, history is a mission. They know its value for future generations. They dismissed my curiosity with a simple: 'Harpenden is well connected to London, which is why many people have always holed up here... even spies.'

This might be true, but too many coincidences do not go unnoticed. And there was actually one more. And as Agatha Christie used to say: 'Three coincidences are a proof.'

Chapter 4

No 95 Batford Prisoner of War Camp

There was already a special bond between Harpenden and Italy during the Second World War, as several Italian prisoners were held in the town between 1943 and 1948. A common thread later also existed between Jicky and her adopted country, not forgetting, also, that her father later married a woman of Italian origin in his second marriage.

In 1942, after the British successes in North Africa, there were thousands of Italian prisoners, and camps were needed to house them. In January 1943 the War Office compiled a list of possible sites in Britain (the threat of invasion had passed) and at the beginning of February told the Harpenden Urban District Council that they intended to requisition a site at Batford, to the north of Common Lane, and commence immediately to build a prisoner of war camp.

The council raised no objection, asking only that it should not encroach on to the council's allotment site, and that it should remain only for the duration of the war. There were not many houses in Batford at that time, and the council pointed out that the sewage system would need enlarging. The camp opened before the system was ready, and toilet arrangements for the first few weeks were rather primitive.

Italian Prisoners

No 95 POW Camp, Batford, opened in May 1943 for Italian prisoners, who were originally housed in tents which were gradually replaced by huts. It accommodated about 600 men. In September 1943 the Italian government signed a peace treaty with the Allies, and shortly afterwards declared war on Germany. This altered the status of the Italians. Although still prisoners, they would be granted certain privileges and better treatment. In July 1944 the camp was re-designated as an Italian Labour Battalion Camp. The men were employed mainly on local farms. In November 1944 the Italians were moved out: some into hostels, and some were lodged at the farms where they were working.[46]

Later, friendships were formed between the Italian prisoners and the inhabitants of Harpenden. Drawings by an Italian man, Pietro Galli, from Viareggio, were found and donated to the town. The website of the Harpenden Local History society provides further information:

'FOR REMEMBER'

Drawings by an Italian PoW in Harpenden in 1944

Squad M.S.9 – Credit: *Scanned from original donated by Alan Marshall*

We have been donated a set of five small, postcard-sized drawings made by an Italian Prisoner of War, Galli Pietro, when he was living at the Batford PoW camp in 1944. He evidently gave them to people who befriended him during his stay in Harpenden, and we are hoping to track down more information about Pietro Galli.

Maybe there are still relatives in his home town of Viareggio. Maybe he was remembering familiar scenes, including Carnival in Venice perhaps. And what was the team of PoWs building?

We hope these drawings may evoke memories in Harpenden families who were living near the camp.[47]

This is a beautiful insight into how Italian prisoners were treated in the town of Harpenden during those difficult years of the war.

Chapter 5

Another 'Enigma' Cracked by a British Engineer

Anthony Piercey, an English engineer, had a beautiful house in Sirolo. Known in the Conero Riviera town as Tony, he spent his days in this residence on Via Molini for many years, and was often spotted when he was out and about in his bright red Audi A3.

Born on 5 November 1929 in Hammersmith, Anthony Piercey was a native of Overton, Hampshire, England as he proudly put it. At the beginning of the Second World War he was briefly evacuated to Wiltshire, where his grandfather owned an idyllic cottage in the village of Wilton, but returned home when he had to start secondary school and attended Isleworth Grammar School. During the war, his school and the local area suffered from German bombing, and it was these early experiences that created a lifelong fascination with anything war-related.[48]

Even then, he followed every action closely. He was obsessed with the encrypted broadcasts that BBC Radio made to provide confidential information to British agents operating in France or other nations under Nazi occupation. He strove to interpret them with the fervent insight of a boy. 'Out of the blue,' he remembered, 'the BBC would throw out seemingly mundane messages, like "milk must be sent..." and we in England guessed it was coded information for our soldiers and secret agents abroad.'

Upon leaving school at 18, he attended night school where he studied engineering and draughtsmanship. Having become a radar and aircraft design engineer, he was called up for National Service with the Royal Air Force. He later created a world-leading company that produced electric blind slats, designed by him, especially for large museums and art galleries. In 1983 he received the British Design Award for his innovative lighting control design, before his love for the Conero Riviera led him to buy his house in Via Molini, where he stayed until his death in November 2020 at the age of 91. Anthony Piercey loved history and spent whole days reading. He knew everything about the Second World War and Napoleon, and for those lucky people who were able to meet him, he gave valuable lessons that are also valid for today.

Anthony was a friend of Jicky's, often buying silverware and other unique pieces for her antique shop in Numana when he went back to England. Anthony's wife would lend Jicky books and she, in turn, would go shopping with her in nearby Porto Civitanova. Anthony knew Paolo, Jicky's partner, and also knew all about her previous husband in Paris, Jean Juvénal.

Jicky and Anthony were similar in their clear pride in being British. Both were united in the same stubbornness and only quarrelled once for trivial reasons, when Anthony had been late for an appointment at Jicky's house because of his English guests who wanted to visit. They did not speak to each other for years.

Only to Anthony had Jicky told of how she had escaped from the Gestapo in Paris after she had been captured and tortured in Fresnes prison. Jicky had always been reticent in her accounts of her activities as an SIS agent, but Anthony had succeeded, through his insistence, in breaking through her defensive wall and grasping the secret that had brought her salvation. He had cracked the enigma that was Jicky.

Anthony said that Jicky was interrogated by the Gestapo on the day of her arrest, despite being in an advanced stage of pregnancy. She was also tortured. Jicky had finally let herself go by confiding in her English friend, who shared the same passion for the Conero Riviera. He was the exception. All she revealed to everyone else was that the Gestapo had thrown her to the floor of a cold cell. Nothing more.

When Anthony asked her how she had broken free from the Nazi grip, Jicky candidly revealed to him that she had been in possession of a forged Irish identity card. We do not know how she obtained this document. Indeed, de Gaulle's Free France group, like all Resistance groups, provided their militants with false passports. Or maybe she got it through the SIS? There is, however, an Irish link as to how she might have been in possession of such a document.

Ireland had remained neutral during Second World War. On 19 February 1939, Taoiseach Éamon de Valera announced that the Irish Free State would be neutral if war broke out. When Britain and France declared war on Germany later that year, on 3 September, he made an announcement through radio broadcast to the people of Ireland, affirming the policy of neutrality and declaring that: '... With our history, with our experience of the last war and with a part of our country still unjustly severed from us, we felt that no other decision and no other policy was possible...'

According to a BBC report, there were other reasons why Ireland remained neutral, one of which was that neutrality was a way of showing the country's independence from Britain. Ireland was also not equipped to fight a war because its army was small and its weak economy meant money was too scarce to be spent on military action. De Valera feared that supporting the war would split the government and country, and as other countries, such as the USA, had declared their neutrality in 1939, Ireland was encouraged to follow their example.

Although many people in Ireland sympathised with the Allied cause, the majority of the Irish population wanted neutrality because it was a British, not an Irish, war.[49] However, according to MI5 files released in January 1999, Ireland was far from neutral. Indeed, such was the level of contact between the British and Irish governments on intelligence matters that their correspondence became known as the Dublin Link.

With Britain's encouragement, once Ireland had established a counterespionage department under the control of the Department of Defence in 1938, personal relations between British and Irish intelligence officers were 'extremely friendly', despite the 'strict political control' exerted upon the Irish department in Dublin. When the war began, MI5 generally found itself playing the role of 'persuader' when gleaning information from Irish intelligence on German activity. The continuation of the Dublin Link (between MI5 and the Department of Defence) was, as far as MI5 could establish, 'entirely dependent' on the political relationship between the two governments. The security service noted, however, that when the Taoiseach, Mr de Valera, declared Ireland's neutrality at the outset of the war, he added a rider that he would not allow Ireland to be used as a base for operations against Britain. From Britain this position was seen to provide Ireland with the political justification for Irish co-operation with Britain on counterespionage and security matters.

When de Valera secured the withdrawal of British garrisons from Ireland's ports in 1938, Britain realised its soldiers in Ireland had been spared 'inevitable' German air attacks, which could have rendered Ireland's neutrality untenable.

Increased goodwill between the two countries, which was due in part to de Valera being taken into the confidence of the British government, safeguarded the work of the Irish section in collecting information about German activity in Ireland. Northern Ireland, too, was a platform for MI5 and MI6 activity during the war as the security services kept a watchful eye on the activities of the IRA, which they feared would betray sensitive military or strategic economic information to Germany.

In 1931, MI5 established contact with the RUC (Royal Ulster Constabulary), which was already passing information about 'revolutionary and seditious' activity in Northern Ireland to MI6. MI5 discussed in great detail the RUC's shortcomings in providing information about 'aliens' operating in the North. 'As far as is known, no one on the RUC staff had any knowledge of German or was familiar with German names...'[50]

This proves that British and Irish intelligence were collaborating secretly together during the Second World War despite the Irish having declared neutrality.

The SOE and SIS connection with Irish intelligence is further confirmed in a report by E. O'Halpin entitled '"Toys" and "Whispers" in "16-land": SOE and Ireland, 1940–1942'. The article's aim was to:

> Explore SOE plans to organise stay behind parties in neutral Ireland in cooperation with Irish army officers, in anticipation of a successful German invasion, as well as efforts to prepare for sabotage operations and to plant rumours through its agent Roddy Keith, and later through the British press attache John Betjeman. SOE's ambitions were opposed both by MI5 and SIS. MI5 wished to protect its own links with Irish intelligence, while SIS feared for the security of its covert Irish networks (which in fact were already penetrated). The consequent rows drew in C, Sir Frank Nelson, and other senior figures. They were resolved by Churchill, who felt that to provide the Irish with war material would only encourage them in their neutrality policy. His verdict was taken as an instruction to SOE to quit Ireland.[51]

A further report in the same publication addresses some of the issues that arose surrounding the SOE's operations in Ireland:

> These involved both preparations for sabotage and for irregular warfare, and schemes for the dissemination of 'whispers', that is manufactured rumours, in Ireland.

> Because of her strategic position in the Atlantic, and her open border with the United Kingdom, Ireland was an obvious candidate for the early attentions of British clandestine warfare agencies.

Thanks to this report, it is clear how deep the connection between British and Irish intelligence was.

It is possible that Jicky had had a fake Irish passport and was able to save her life through Irish intelligence collaborating with the SIS. While Irish diplomats were more likely to have had access to documents and official stamps, French intelligence, in collaboration with the SOE, had access to their forgery department. MI6 may well have been involved, too. No proof exists, however, of the provenance of Jicky's forged Irish document.

Nevertheless, the fact is that thanks to forged Irish papers, Jicky was one of the few British women secret agents to survive after being arrested by the Gestapo.

Chapter 6

Anthony Piercey's Revelations

On the day my book, *L'Angelo di Churchill*, was presented in Sirolo in August 2020, Anthony Piercey had candidly raised his hand at the end of the speeches, during a Q&A with the audience. Everyone was a little stunned. He had started calmly, in Italian with a strong British accent, telling of his friendship with Jicky – he did not know her real name was Hazel – and that every time he returned to England, he bought vintage silverware for her antique shop in Numana. Then the bombshell dropped. Jicky had confessed to him that she had false Irish identity papers and that since Ireland was not at war, the Irish could not be arrested or detained in prisons for espionage. According to Anthony, this was the real reason why Jicky was one of the very few British agents to escape from the clutches of the Nazis.

Given her acumen and readiness to come up with a Plan B, however, qualities that Prime Minister Churchill so enjoyed for his secret agents, if this was true, surely Jicky would have tried to speak with an Irish accent?

Visiting Anthony privately at home, I discovered the brutal thing he dared not tell in front of everyone in the square in Sirolo on the day of the book presentation. When Jicky was interrogated by the Nazis in the last stages of her pregnancy, she was completely stripped naked. Only to him, a fellow British citizen, did she confess that they had undressed her completely.

When I asked if he thought she had been raped despite her baby bump, he gave no answer. He did not know. He merely said that she was tortured, without knowing in what form the torture took place.

They tortured her because at first the Gestapo did not believe that she was Irish but British, when they received the tip-off. It took her a long time to convince them and only proved it by producing that precious forgery, the forged document from the government of Ireland. The most life-saving forgery that granted her freedom.

Jicky had also told him details about her husband, Jean Juvénal, whom she had met and married after the war and who had recognised her son as his. Juvénal was also a fine art expert and owned a rich collection of paintings. Jicky had helped him in the organisation and management of his works of art, as well as in the office. Indeed, she had been such a valuable collaborator that he proposed marriage to her.

Chapter 7

A Plaque for Jicky

It was an immense effort to have the town of Sirolo recognise Jicky for her sacrifices in France during the Second World War. With the hope that at least in the future Britain can do justice and honour with a tribute to this brave and strong woman, I decided to fight my personal battle from Italy. Voltaire spoke of the 'justness of justice'. Here it was completely absent. As was the principle of gratitude.

Leaving her memory to oblivion was almost disgraceful, an outrage against such an important figure. Following Voltaire's beliefs, I wanted to fight so that Jicky at least received local recognition in her hometown in Sirolo. After all, there were many unknown figures like her who had saved Europe from the Nazi-fascist yoke.

Finally, after two years, the answer came from the Cultural Circle of Sirolo. They had agreed to purchase a precious marble plaque that would be affixed to the house where Jicky had lived for so many years. The plaque would be finely crafted by master marble workers from Recanati, with an inscription in a beautiful royal blue.

The first and only award in Italy dedicated to a secret agent of the British government, the ceremony for the unveiling of the historical plaque took place on 7 May 2022 which, coincidentally, was the same day of the German unconditional surrender in 1945. During the event, a diplomat from the British embassy in Rome, Cameron Ballester, paid a heartfelt tribute to Jicky by highlighting her courage and hoping that she would be 'an inspiration to all', before continuing to highlight the friendship between the English and Italian people. Pascale Mussard, the great-granddaughter of the Hermès family from Paris, who had flown in for the occasion, spoke about when they had lived in the same house together in Paris and their special relationship. It was a touching intervention and helped to reveal Jicky's human side, the sweet and tender one, beyond the haughty appearance of her strong character. From Pascale's words one could understood the affection and respect she had for this great woman.

Professor Marta Marchetti, the director of the Winston Churchill Museum in Montemaggiore al Metauro (the only museum in Italy dedicated to the British Premier, located where he went to observe the 8th British Army arrive from Montecassino in August 1944), highlighted the importance of celebrating and remembering, especially in this time of war, women like Jicky who had contributed to freedom and democracy. She then quoted an inscription in the Casa del Mutilato in Genoa, a home for war invalids: 'War is the lesson of history that people never remember enough.'

The Sirolo band and choir solemnly performed the national anthems, 'God Save The Queen' and 'Mameli's Hymn', and many people flocked to the event, including several Britons as well as locals, and Jicky's friends from Bologna. Today, it is wonderful to see tourists queuing up in the summer to admire the marble plaque to this proud Englishwoman. The younger ones, meanwhile, queue up for a selfie.

Thanks to this plaque, Jicky's memory will live on in history forever.

Bibliography

Beevor, Antony & Cooper, Artemis, *PARIS After the Liberation 1944-1949*, Penguin Books, 1995.
Camus, Albert, *The Plague*, Editions Gallimard, 1947, Bompiani Edition, Milan.
Chanel, Gerri, *Saving Mona Lisa*, Icon Books, London, 2018.
Crowdy, Terry, *SOE: Churchill's Secret Agents*, Shire Publications Ltd, Oxford, 2016.
De Gaulle, Charles, *Memorie della Speranza, Il rinnovamento: 1958-1962*, Rizzoli, 1970.
Dragoni, Giorgio, Fichera, Giuseppe, *Fountain Pens: History and Design, Penne* stilografiche, Storia e Design, Mondadori, Milan, 1997.
Foulkes, Nicholas, *Bernard Buffet: The Invention of The Modern Mega-Artist*, Arrow Books, 2017.
Fry, Helen, *MI9*, Yale University Press New Haven and London, 2021.
Guéhenno, Jean, *Diary of the Dark Years 1940-1947*, Oxford University Press, New York, translated into English in 2014.
Hebborn Eric, *Italico per Italiani: Un Moderno Trattato di Calligrafia*, Angelo Colla Editore, 2004.
Kahn, David, *The Codebreakers*, Mondadori, 1969.
Maggi, Mario, *Montefano nelle sue tradizioni popolari*, Municipality of Montefano, Fondazione Cassa di Risparmio della Provincia di Macerata, 2003.
McDougall, Christopher, *Natural Born Heroes*, Profile Books LTD, London, 2015.
Nietzsche, *The Gay Science* (section 299).
O'Connor, Bernard, *Churchill's Angels*, Amberley Publishing, Gloucestershire, 2012.
O' Connor, Bernard, *Churchill's School for Saboteurs Station 17*, Amberly Publishing, Stroud, Gloucestershire, 2013.

O'Connor, Bernard, *Operation Ebensburg, SOE's Austrian 'Bonzos' and the Rescue of Looted European Art*, Lulu.com, 2018.
Read Piers Paul, The Dreyfus Affair: The Story of the Most Infamous Miscarriage of Justice in French History, Bloomsbury Publishing PLC, 2013.
Roland, Paul, *Nazi Women: The Attraction of Evil*, Arcturus Holdings Limited, 2014.
Shakespeare, William, *Henry V.*
Shakespeare, William, *A Midsummer Night's Dream.*
Teillard, Ania, *Soul and Handwriting: A Treatise on Graphology based on Analytical Psycology*, Maurice Delamain, Presentation by Franca Mühlmann, Bollati Boringhieri, 1997.
Walker, Robyn, *The Women Who Spied for Britain*, Amberley Publishing, Gloucestershire, 2015.

Websites:

https://www.legacy.com/us/obituaries/nytimes/name/charles-lieber-obituary?id=12572171 Accessed: 25/4/2025

http://www.bbc.com/news/uk-northern-ireland-11400814 Accessed: 24/10/2010

https://www.oxfordreference.com/view/10.1093/oi/authority.20110803095943133 Accessed: 3/3/2022

RAF Special Duties Squadrons during WW2 – Alan Malcher Accessed: 13/9/2024

https://www.servicehistorique.sga.defense.gouv.fr/centres-shd/vincennes-centre-historique-des-archives Accessed: 20/6/2022

https://www.larousse.fr/encyclopedie/personnage/Andr%C3%A9_Dewavrin_dit_le_colonel_Passy/137207 Accessed: 14/7/2022

Claude Gerard JUVENAL Base de données des décès de l'insee - GénéaFrance (geneafrance.com) Accessed: 6/7/2022

https://heritage.statueofliberty.org/passenger-details/ Accessed: 6/7/2022

https://www.france-libre.net/comite-fl-uruguay/ Accessed: 20/7/2022

https://www.archivioapostolicovaticano.va/content/dam/aav/documenti/CAV_52_vol1.pdf Accessed: 13/9/2024

Lager – Museo Nazionale Dell'Internamento (museodellinternamento.it) Accessed: 17/9/2024 https://museodellinternamento.it/lager/ Accessed: 17/9/2024

https://scholarworks.indianapolis.iu.edu/server/api/core/bitstreams/aa20f6b1-f74e-4739-a96e-6b19e1c81578/content Accessed: 25/4/2025

https://www.harpenden-history.org.uk/harpenden-history/topics-cms/wartime_-_second_world_war_wwii/pows-and-batford-camp/no_95_batford_prisoner_of_war_camp Accessed: 18/9/2024

https://www.harpenden-history.org.uk/harpenden-history/topics-cms/wartime_-_second_world_war_wwii/pows-and-batford-camp/for_remember Accessed: 18/9/2024

https://www.bbc.co.uk/bitesize/guides/zty47p3/revision/1, 2/7/2024

https://www.irishtimes.com/culture/how-neutral-ireland-helped-britain-win-the-war-1.1258712 Accessed: 2/7/2024

https://doi.org/10.1080/02684520008432625 Accessed:2/7/2024

MI14 Pigeon Service to Occupied Europe (arcre.com) Accessed: 1/7/2024

https://everloved.com/life-of/anthony-piercey/obituary/ Accessed: 25/4/2023

Endnotes

1. The section of Britain's military intelligence responsible for the security of the country's overseas interests. Part of its role was collecting military, economic and political intelligence of the country. This was obtained overtly from books, journals, newspapers, magazines, the radio and television and direct contact with people who knew the sort of information Britain needed. In some cases, agents paid for information and in others, the intelligence was obtained covertly. Wireless messages were intercepted, recorded and translated. Buildings were broken into and documents photographed using miniature cameras - just like in Ian Fleming's novels.
2. Helen Fry, *MI9*, Yale University Press New Haven and London, 2021, p.35.
3. The earliest SIS agents parachuted into France were provided with two pigeons and a small bag of grain. The birds were put inside socks which had a hole cut in the toe where the bird's head would poke through. The first bird was released when the agent landed in the field. It would fly back across the English Channel to its loft above the Station Commander's garage at Bletchley Park, Buckinghamshire. This mansion had been purchased by Stewart Menzies, Head of MI6 to be an agent training school. However, the British Code and Cypher Section was relocated to Bletchley Park following the outbreak of war and another mansion, Brickendonbury Manor, Hertfordshire, was acquired for agent training. When the bird entered the loft, it stepped on a board which caused a bell to ring. The loftman came and retrieved the number of the bird which he passed on to the MI6 agent's handler to let him know that the agent had landed safely. The second pigeon was used to send a message written on thin paper and inserted into the container attached to its leg. It contained the coordinates of the field

which the agent had identified as suitable for a Westland Lysander to land, pick up the agent and fly him - or her - back to Britain. Suggested dates and times were included. When the pigeon returned to Bletchley Park, the message would be retrieved by the loftman, who would ring the police. A motorcycle courier would be sent to collect it and take it to Wing House in Piccadilly, London, the headquarters of MI14, the British Pigeon Service. The Royal Air Force's Special Duties Squadron would be asked to send a Lysander pilot to pick up the waiting agent. Later in the war, pigeons were dropped by parachute in the hope that pro-Allied civilians would find them and send back intelligence on the piece of paper inserted into the leg container.

4. http://www.bbc.com/news/uk-northern-ireland-11400814, 24/10/2010.
5. Piers Paul Read, *The Dreyfus Affair: The Story of the Most Infamous Miscarriage of Justice in French History*, Bloomsbury Publishing, 2013.
6. Eric Hebborn, *Italico per Italiani*, (Italic for Italians), Angelo Colla Editore, 2004.
7. Giorgio Dragoni, Giuseppe Fichera, *Fountain Pens: History and Design, (Penne stilografiche: Storia e Design)*, Mondadori, Milan, 1997.
8. Ania Teillard, *The Soul and Writing*, Maurice Delamain, Presentation by Franca Mühlmann, original edition, Bollati Boringhieri, 1997.
9. Bernard O'Connor, *Churchill's Angels*, Amberley Publishing, 2012, Gloucestershire, p. 35.
10. Even today MI6 will neither confirm nor deny the existence of an officer in their employment or an activity they are thought to have been involved in.
11. Crowdy, Terry, *SOE: Churchill's Secret Agents*, Shire Publications Ltd, Oxford, 2016.
12. Robyn Walker, *The Women Who Spied for Britain*, Amberley Publishing, Gloucestershire, 2015, p. 23-24.
13. FANY officers were also allowed to carry a weapon.
14. https://scholarworks.indianapolis.iu.edu/server/api/core/bitstreams/aa20f6b1-f74e-4739-a96e-6b19e1c81578/content, 25/4/2025.
15. Paul Roland, *Nazi Women: The Attraction of Evil*, Arcturus Holdings Limited, 2014.

16. Charles de Gaulle, *Memoirs of Hope, The Renewal: 1958-1962*, (*Memorie della Speranza, il Rinnovamento: 1958-1962*), Rizzoli, 1970, p. 49.
17. William Shakespeare, *A Midsummer Night's Dream*, Act 1, Scene 1.
18. David Kahn, *The Codebreakers, (La Guerra dei Codici)*, Mondadori, 1969, p. 9.
19. Ibid, p. 14.
20. William Shakespeare, *Henry V*, Act Two, Scene Two.
21. David Kahn, *The Codebreakers, (La Guerra dei Codici), Mondadori, 1969, p. 321.*
22. All numbers next to words or consonants have been changed to avoid spreading any secret codes not yet declassified by the British government.
23. Addresses are omitted specifically for privacy reasons.
24. Keith Varty Obituary, *British Vogue*, 12 April 2019.
25. *Mario Maggi, Montefano nelle sue tradizioni popolari* (*Montefano in its Popular Traditions*), Preface, Municipality of Montefano, Fondazione Cassa di Risparmio della Provincia di Macerata, 2003.
26. Alessandra Ferretti, *Jicky*, poem, 2010.
27. Robyn Walker, *The Women Who Spied for Britain*, Amberley Publishing, Gloucestershire, 2015, foreword.
28. Albert Camus, *The Plague*, Editions Gallimard, 1947, Bompiani Edition, Milan, p. 54.
29. Ibid p. 55.
30. Ibid.
31. Ibid p. 56.
32. Ibid, p. 235.
33. Jean Guéhenno, *Diary of the Dark Years 1940-1947*, Oxford University Press, New York, translated into English in 2014.
34. Gerri Chanel, *Saving Mona Lisa*, Icon Books, London, 2018.
35. Bernard O'Connor, *Operation Ebensburg, SOE's Austrian 'Bonzos' and the Rescue of Looted European Art*, Lulu.com, 2018.
36. https://www.oxfordreference.com/view/10.1093/oi/authority.20110803095943133 3/3/2022.
37. Nicholas Foulkes, *Bernard Buffet: The Invention of The Modern Mega-Artist*, Arrow Books, Great Britain, 2017.

38. Antony Beevor & Artemis Cooper, *Paris After the Liberation 1944-1949*, Penguin Books, 1995, Great Britain.
39. Nietzsche, *The Gay Science* (section 299).
40. Winston Churchill, 'We shall fight on the beaches' speech, 4 June 1940, House of Commons.
41. Christopher McDougall, *Natural Born Heroes*, Profile Books LTD, London, 2015.
42. Antony Beevor and Artemis Cooper, *Paris After the Liberation 1944-1949*, Penguin Books, 1995, Great Britain.
43. RAF No. 138 Special Duties Squadron was responsible for dropping agents, weapons, sabotage equipment and other stores by parachute inside occupied Europe and flew as far as Poland and Yugoslavia from RAF Tempsford. There was also a detachment serving the Middle East. RAF Special Duties Squadrons during WW2 – Alan Malcher 13/9/2024.
44. Bernard O' Connor, *Churchill's School For Saboteurs: Station 17*, Amberly Publishing, Stroud, Gloucestershire, 2013.
45. Part of the British government's attempt to determine who would be eligible for conscription in time of war.
46. https://www.harpenden-history.org.uk/harpenden-history/topics-cms/wartime_-_second_world_war_wwii/pows-and-batford-camp/no_95_batford_prisoner_of_war_camp 18/9/2024.
47. https://www.harpenden-history.org.uk/harpenden-history/topics-cms/wartime_-_second_world_war_wwii/pows-and-batford-camp/for_remember 18/9/2024.
48. https://everloved.com/life-of-anthony-piercey/obituary/, 25 April 2023.
49. https://www.bbc.co.uk/bitesize/guides/zty47p3/revision/1, 2/7/2024.
50. https://www.irishtimes.com/culture/how-neutral-ireland-helped-britain-win-the-war-1.1258712, 2/7/2024.
51. https://doi.org/10.1080/02684520008432625, 2/7/2024.

Index

Anne, Princess Royal, 105
Artias, Philippe, 43
Ashenden/Ashendon, Margaret Emily, 161, 164
Avenue Foch, 20-1, 143

Baker, Josephine, 140-1
Ballester, Cameron, 182
BBC, 99, 115, 133, 174, 176
Bergé, Pierre, 34, 119-20
Bletchley Park, 18, 51-2, 170
Blow, Percival, 168
Bossi, Umberto, 11, 76, 134
Brussels, 4, 6-7, 18, 19, 34, 53, 123, 148, 158-9, 164
Buffet, Bernard, 34, 45, 47, 85, 116-21

Calligraphic/handwriting analyses, 4, 7, 10-16, 18, 51, 58-9, 88, 90, 100, 106, 137, 169-70
Camp, 144, 154
Camus, Albert, 112-13, 116
Catherine, Princess of Wales, 52
Churchill's Angels, 4, 18, 105
Conero Mountain, Riviera, 40, 42-3, 44, 46, 48, 55, 60, 77-8, 101, 104, 106, 174-5

Corbidge, John, 43
Cornil-Frerrot, Sylvain, 129
Cryptography/cryptology/ cryptographic analysis, 52-3
Cryptanalysis unit, 51, 52-3
Cultural Circle of Sirolo, 105, 182

D-Day, 26, 115
Dansey, Claude Edward, 5
De Gaulle, Charles, 7, 26, 27-9, 33, 38, 100, 114, 132-5, 138-9, 142, 148, 149, 151-3, 156
De Gaulle's Free France Foundation, 129, 143
De Gaulle's Free France Groups, 30, 130, 136, 138-9, 140, 145, 152, 156, 176
De Valera, Éamon, 176-7
Della Valle, Diego, (Mr Tod's), 49-50
Dreyfus Affair, 12, 168-70
Dreyfus, Alfred, 12-13, 169
Dublin Link, 176-7
Dumas, Pierre-Alexis, 37
Dunkirk, 27-8, 138-9
Durand, Lucien, 129-31, 132, 136-9, 156
Durand, Lucienne, 59, 129, 140-2

Enigma code/programme/machine, 52, 58, 170
Esterhazy, Ferdinand, 12-13, 168-70

French Defence Historical Service at Vincennes, 125, 129-31, 146
Ford, Tom, 78
Fresnes prison, 21, 30, 175

Gaullist, 139, 149, 151
Gestapo, 20, 22, 30-2, 82, 92, 124, 129, 140, 144, 147, 175, 179, 181
Goverrment Code and Cypher School/Section, 51
Graphic analyses, essay, investigation, 13-14, 52-4, 62, 90, 100
Guéhenno, Jean, 113, 134
Guerrand-Hermès, Myriam, 37
Hari Mata, 24
Harpenden, Hertfordshire, 3, 158-73
Harpenden & District Local History Society, 173
Hazel, Katherine Nancy, 148
Hebrew Publishing Company, 7
Hermès-Dumas, 33-8
Hermès, Thierry, 33, 37
Hermès, Charles-Émile, 33
Hitler, Adolf, 25, 28, 81-2, 111-2, 114-5, 126, 133
IRA, 177
Ireland, 176-8, 180-1

Irish intelligence, 176-9, 180-1
Italian PoWs, 156, 172-3

Juvénal, Claude, 30, 33, 37, 41, 45, 58-9, 62, 85-6, 96-7, 104, 123-4, 129-30, 140-1, 143, 151-3
Juvénal, Jean, 33, 143, 175, 181
Jung, Carl Gustav, 15, 123

Keen, David, 160
Khan, Noor Inayat, 22
Kirkwick Lodge, Harpenden, 163-4

Lamarr, Hedy, 53
Lieber, Charles D., 6-7, 59-60, 102, 123, 158
Linacre, Nicola, 165

Maggi, Mario, 93
Magritte, 34, 85
Maquis, 26, 109
Marchetti, Marta, 183
Menzies, Stewart, 51
Metreweli, Blaise, 4
MI5, 5, 63, 176-8
MI6, 3-7, 14, 51, 92, 105, 177, 179
MI14, 8
Mussard Siegrist, Pascale, 37-8, 124, 182-3

No 95 POW Camp, Batford, 172-3
Nacht und Nebel, 21-2
National Archives, The, 105, 154-5
Negulesco, Jean, 118
Numana, 42-3, 48-9, 61, 78, 84, 175, 180

OSS, 18, 134

Paolini, Paolo, 41-9, 60, 62, 69, 79-80, 86, 92, 94-8, 100, 103, 175
Parrott, Diana, 160, 167
Passy, André Dewavrin, 149-50
Pétain, Philippe, 109, 114, 133, 151
Picasso, Pablo, 43, 117-20, 139
Piercey, Anthony ('Tony'), 174-5, 180-1
Plaque for Jicky, 182-3
Porquerolles, Hyères, 36-7, 39, 43, 120

RAF, 8, 19, 25, 144
Random House, 6
Rimington, Stella, 5, 63, 93
Robuste, Marie, 148
Ross, Rosemary, 166-7
Rothamsted Manor and Rothamsted Research, 167, 170
RUC, Royal Ulster Constabulary, 177

Saint Laurent, Yves, 34, 119-20
Sbrava, David, 131, 146
Shakespeare, William, 40, 53, 75, 83
Siegrist, Pierre, 37
Simenon, Georges, 37, 120

Sinclair, Hugh 'Quex', 51
Sirolo, Italy, 9, 36, 38, 40, 42-50, 54, 57, 61, 70, 77-80, 85-6, 88, 92, 94-5, 97-8, 100-106, 120, 144, 165-6, 167, 174, 180, 182-3
Smith Sydney Herbert, 161, 164
Smith-Cumming, Mansfield George, 51
St. Albans, 158, 161, 164, 168

Teillard, Ania, 15-6, 123
Trump, Donald, 14
Turing, Alan, 58

UN, 41

Varty, Dorothy, 77-9, 92, 99, 123-4
Varty, Keith, 77-8
Venables, Edward, 147
Venables, Margareth Hazel, 146-7
Villa Dancourt, Paris, 59, 140-1
Villa Wolkonsky, 21
Vogel, Gerard, 129-32, 138-40, 143-4, 151-6

Winston Churchill Museum, Montemaggiore, 183

Younger, Alex, 4